Advance Praise for *Force Decisions*

Rory Miller pulls no punches in this hard-hitting look at the sometimes controversial topic of Use of Force and related force issues. He's going to push some people's buttons with this book, and that's good, because some people need their buttons pushed. I'd like to see every attorney read this book and just maybe it would eliminate, or at least reduce, the number of excessive force charges against officers who did nothing wrong. Miller does an excellent job of weaving legalities, moral issues, and experience into a practical look at force issues for both law enforcement offers and citizens they protect. I agree with Miller's first hard truth, "The only defense against evil, violent people is good people who are more skilled at violence." And I sincerely hope that people will read this comprehensive text and better understand why those sworn to serve and protect must use physical force to stop evil, and appreciate the decision to use such force, that officers must make under extreme conditions. I commend and thank Miller for writing this important addition to the literature related to violence and law enforcement. Superb job!

Alain Burrese, J.D., former U.S. Army 2nd Infantry Division Scout Sniper School instructor and author of *Hard-Won Wisdom From the School of Hard Knocks*, and the DVDs *Hapkido Hoshinsul*, *Streetfighting Essentials*, *Hapkido Cane*, and the *Lock On: Joint Lock Essentials* series

As always, Miller's work delivers far more than he promises. On the surface, this book is designed to explain to civilians how the thin blue line that protects them approaches the use of force. It accomplishes that task admirably. Having read this book, civilians will have a baseline understanding about the difficult and life-changing decisions law enforcement personnel make every day on their behalf. But this book is far more than an introduction to decisions that, to most civilians, will seem far-removed from their sheltered realities. At its heart, this book is an exploration of the mindset of both those sworn to protect and serve and of those from whom they protect us. For most of us, both perspectives will seem like alien worlds. To my mind, Miller's guided tour through both worldviews is the most valuable aspect of this book, and it will be the reason I recommend it to my friends and family.

Rob Crowley, attorney and former Major, United States Army Special Forces

"Police brutality! You can't do this! I know my rights!" is something police officers hear almost every day. But unfortunately, the people who say this often forget that the law not only gives them rights; it also gives them duties. You don't get one without the other. Neither can you claim your rights while refusing to uphold your duties. It's this disconnect that creates such problems in today's society and lands people in jail or with heavy fines to pay when it all could have been avoided . . .

In this book, Rory Miller gives you the information you need to understand what "Use of Force" is and how police officers follow procedures to enforce the law. Not only that, he also explains the logic behind them as well as all the legal aspects involved. You'll read not only the theory but also numerous real-life examples that illustrate how it works. As a result, you'll not only know your rights as a citizen but also your duties and both how and why police officers enforce them.

Do yourself a favor and read this book. You'll get the information you hope you'll never have to use, but will find invaluable the moment you absolutely need it.

Wim Demeere, martial artists, author of *The Fighters Body*

When you give somebody a badge, guns, a taser, pepper spray, and a baton, there needs to be a clear policy laid out as to when it is appropriate to use these tools. How and why the police apply force is something most civilians know little or nothing about, save stories they see on the evening news; Rory Miller's book explains this in a way that is both entertaining and informative.

The police are human and sometimes they screw up; mostly when they do, it is because they stepped away from departmental policies designed to protect them and the citizens.

Steve Perry, New York Times Bestselling co-author of Tom Clancy's *Net Force* Series

Force Decisions—A Citizen's Guide **was written for those of us who blissfully go through life** believing we will never have to defend ourselves, will never get into trouble with the law, or will never have to be "interviewed" by a police officer.

Force Decisions will help you understand the world that law police officers must live in, twenty-four hours a day, seven days a week. That a police officer must go *into* danger while the rest of us try to avoid or run *away* from danger.

While reading you will learn much more about yourself.

George Mattson, martial artist, author of *The Way of Karate*

FORCE DECISIONS
A CITIZEN'S GUIDE

FORCE DECISIONS
A CITIZEN'S GUIDE

Understanding How Police Determine Appropriate Use of Force

Rory Miller

YMAA Publication Center, Inc.
Wolfeboro NH USA

YMAA Publication Center, Inc.
PO Box 480
Wolfeboro, NH 03894
800-669-8892 • www.ymaa.com • info@ymaa.com

Paperback edition 978-1-59439-243-6
Ebook edition 978-1-59439-244-3

Cover design by Axie Breen
Editing by Karen Barr Grossman
Photos provided by the author

20200123

Publisher's Cataloging in Publication

Miller, Rory.

Force decisions : a citizen's guide : understanding how police determine appropriate use of force / Rory Miller. —Wolfeboro, NH : YMAA Publication Center, c2012.

p. ; cm.
ISBN: 978-1-59439-243-6 (pbk.) ; 978-1-59439-244-3 (ebk.)
Includes bibliographical references and index.
Summary: This book allows you to 'take' a basic "use of force" police academy class, including training, checks and balances, experience, and review (from both the police and the suspect points of view).—Publisher.

1. Police discretion—United States. 2. Police training—United States. 3. Arrest (Police methods)—United States. 4. Self-defense (Law)—United States. 5. Restraint of prisoners—United States. 6. Justifiable homicide—United States. 7. Violence (Law)—United States. 8. Necessity (Law)—United States. 9. Tort liability of police—United States. 10. Police misconduct—United States. 11. Policecommunity relations—United States. I. Title.
II. Title: Understanding how police determine appropriate use of force.

HV7936.D54 M55 2012 2012933335
363.2/32—dc23 1210

Warning: While self-defense is legal, fighting is illegal. If you don't know the difference you'll go to jail because you aren't defending yourself, you are fighting—or worse. Readers are encouraged to be aware of all appropriate local and national laws relating to self-defense, reasonable force, and the use of weaponry, and act in accordance with all applicable laws at all times. Understand that while legal definitions and interpretations are generally uniform, there are small—but very important—differences from state to state. To stay out of jail, you need to know these differences. Neither the authors nor the publisher assumes any responsibility for the use or misuse of information contained in this book.

Nothing in this document constitutes a legal opinion nor should any of its contents be treated as such. While the authors believe that everything herein is accurate, any questions regarding specific self-defense situations, legal liability, and/or interpretation of federal, state, or local laws should always be addressed by an attorney at law. This text relies on public news sources to gather information on various crimes and criminals described herein. While news reports of such incidences are generally accurate, they are on occasion incomplete or incorrect. Consequently, all suspects should be considered innocent until proven guilty in a court of law.

When it comes to martial arts, self-defense, and related topics, no text, no matter how well written, can substitute for professional, hands-on instruction. These materials should be used **for academic study only**.

Printed in USA.

CONTENTS

ACKNOWLEDGEMENTS

I owe a debt of gratitude to a lot of people.

Loren Christensen, John Lupo, Jean Nichols, Sean Croft, Jim Sheeran, Lawdog MG, Eliel Hernandez, Frank Rodriguez (and the rest of the Pariah Dogs), Edward Raso, Jeff Gaynor, and George Mattson all graciously offered stories for this book. Be safe, all of you.

Most of them also helped with the manuscript, especially pointing out where I went off in my own private language. So did Rick Vogt, Melissa Williams, and Lawrence Kane. Good friends. Okay editors.

Donnla Nic Gearailt graciously offered to serve as a Subject Matter Expert on mental illness. Thank you.

That was about the book. The next is about me:

The officers who initially taught me Use of Force, especially Paul McRedmond (originator of the Three Golden Rules explained in section 1.2) and Ron Bishop, in my opinion, did an outstanding job. They had a truly encyclopedic knowledge of force policy and law, as well as deep experience with application.

Hundreds, if not thousands of officers and criminals over the years have also taught their particular lessons. We were not always friends, but I still thank them.

The indomitable Kami, wise and beautiful, who has held me when I bled or wanted to cry, has kept me sane through everything.

This one's for Mac.

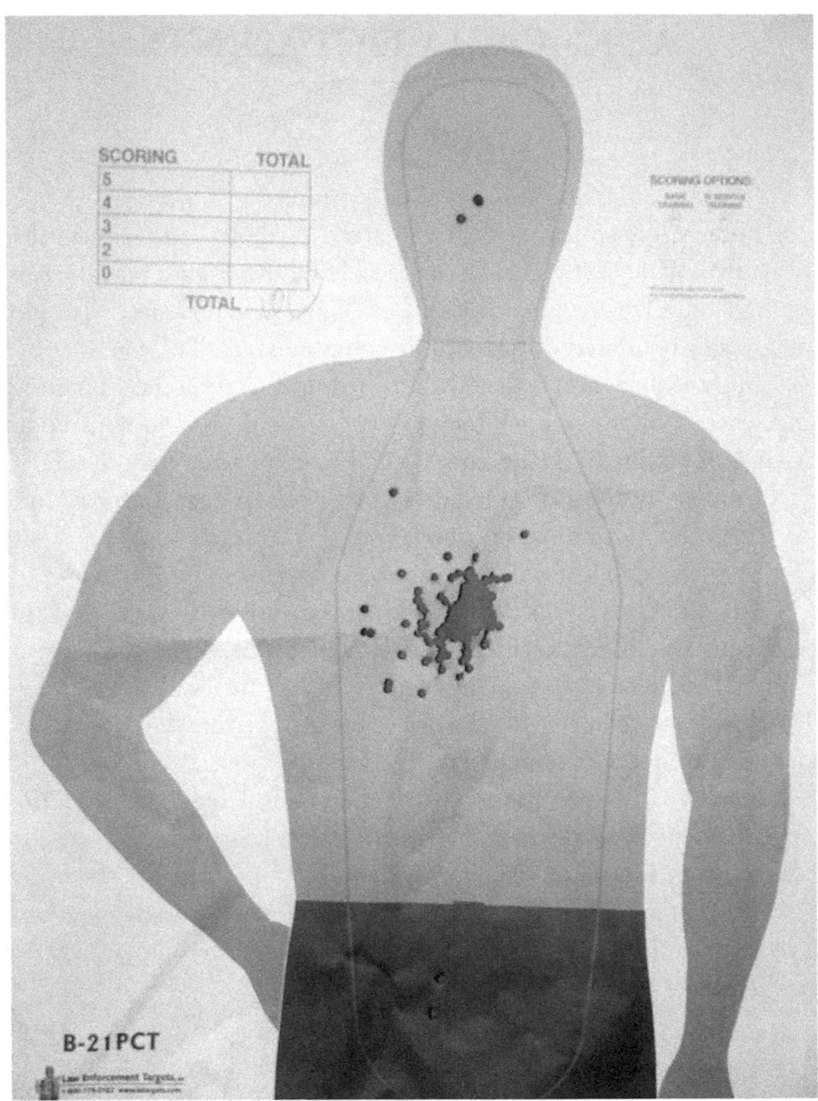
SCORING
TOTAL
5
4
3
2
0
TOTAL
SCORING OPTIONS
B-21PCT
Law Enforcement Targets

INTRODUCTION

This book is a gift, a peace offering. It is an attempt to communicate across a vast gulf in culture and experience, the gulf that exists between the Law Enforcement community and those whom they protect.

Each day, media outlets all over the country describe events where officers use force. Often, the reporters and the citizens question the need for force at all or whether the type and amount of force used was really necessary. Citizens worry that their protectors—with badges, guns, clubs and Tasers®—are caught up in the rush of power, or perhaps giving vent to anger or bigotry.

The officers are frustrated too. Specialists in dealing with a world that is sometimes very dark and very violent, they feel scrutinized. They feel as if their actions are constantly under a microscope, judged by a populace without any experience or training in a very specialized field.

In this book, I want to show you how officers think about force, not only how we are trained to think of it, but also how experience shapes our beliefs and attitudes.

If you are one of the people who believe that officers are thugs and question each and every use of force, I don't want to change you. Let me say that again: I don't want to change you. Sometimes my job requires me to use force on behalf of society, on *your* behalf. That force should be subject to *your* scrutiny.

What I do want, if you have objections, is to have those objections based on facts and not emotion. Most people will have a negative reaction to any violence, and some problems (from child-raising to the boardroom to politics and medicine and . . .) simply don't have an answer that makes everyone comfortable.

You know what you saw or read. You know how that made you feel. The final data that you need to back up your reasonable objections are knowledge of the rules—to understand thoroughly the legal and policy limits as well as the tactical considerations that the professionals understand.

There are truths and perceptions that frame this gulf. First, the perceptions: We have all been taught that peace is an ideal, and that hurting people is wrong. We have also been taught, in an egalitarian society, that what is wrong for one is wrong for all. And what is wrong to do to someone is wrong to do to anyone.

The truth, however, is harsh. It is this: The only defense against evil, violent people is good people who are more skilled at violence.

HARD TRUTH #1

The only defense against evil, violent people is good people who are more skilled at violence.

Throughout history, civilized people faced with people willing to use violence to attain their goals have tried a number of strategies.

Appeasement has failed. The hope that Hitler would be satisfied with Poland and Czechoslovakia only gave him more time to prepare. Bribery has failed, and paying off terrorists to prevent terrorism has been no more effective than Danegeld—money paid to Vikings to stop plundering. Reason and logic could not prevent the Khmer Rouge from killing every educated person in Cambodia. Simply being a good person couldn't dissuade the Inquisition.

Ah, but there is always Gandhi . . .

Not really. Without a relatively free press, a lot of publicity, and an opponent who needed support (both from voters and from trading partners), Gandhi would have quietly disappeared. Where were the Gandhis of Pol Pot's Cambodia, Stalin's Russia, or Ceasescu's Romania? Prague Spring—an attempt by the Czechs to create "socialism with a human face"—was ruthlessly crushed by the soviets.

The ideal of peaceful resistance only works when backed by the big guns of public opinion and economics, and only then if those two things matter to the person or institution that one is trying to change.

This is a hard truth: In a truly totalitarian environment the authorities cannot only kill, but they have control over who finds out about it (communications and the media) and have control over the means to respond (control of economics, the vote and/or personal weapons). When these factors come together the populace is helpless, and the tactics of peaceful resistance result in death, torture, and the disappearance of family members.

HARD TRUTH #2

> *In a truly totalitarian environment where the authorities cannot only kill, but have control over who finds out about it and, have control over the means to respond, the populace is helpless.*

This is the world: The wolf pack tears at a caribou, slashing at hamstrings, tearing out guts. Raw, primal violence. The caribou will run if it can, but if it can't, it will respond as best it can with violence of its own, kicking and goring the pack.

A cat toys with a mouse. The mouse may bite *you* if you try to save it.

Some predators stalk, some run in packs, some lie in ambush. All predators use violence as a strategy, the easiest and safest way to access a resource that they need or want.

Human predators are the same.

If a person can do so safely, it is easier to steal food than to grow it. It is easier to beat the weak into submission than to earn their respect. It is far easier to rape and abandon a woman than it is to raise children. All provided it can be done *safely*. Society, or someone acting on behalf of society, must make that kind of behavior unsafe.

A peaceful individual is ill-prepared to deal with a violent human being. The tactics of the courtroom, the boardroom, or the mediator simply don't work on someone who wants something and has no problem injuring someone to take it. A peaceful society compounds this by allowing the peaceful individuals to believe that their worldview is normal. It is a beautiful ideal but for most of human history, and in many places now, and even within individuals in the most civilized of

> Violence and crime will probably never disappear, for practical reasons. The rarer they become, the less experience and skill potential victims will have to combat them. The less violence and crime happens, the less it factors into planning, and the less people take care to protect themselves.
>
> So the more rare violence is, the more profitable and safe violence becomes.
>
> Crime and violence are usually an *individual advantage*, but they weaken the connections that keep society going and are a *community disadvantage.*

societies, it doesn't hold true. There are people for whom violence is a natural way to get what they want.

Civilized people must come to terms with the fact that only force, or the credible threat of force, could stop a Hitler, a Pol Pot, or a John Dillinger.

It's often been said, "Violence never solved anything." The simple truth is that when you are slammed up against the wall and the knife is at your throat, when a circle of teenagers is kicking you as you curl into a ball on the sidewalk, or when the man walks into your office building or school with a pair of guns and starts shooting—only violence, or the reasonable threat of violence, is going to save your life. In the extreme moment, only force can stop force.

HARD TRUTH #3

In the extreme moment, only force can stop force.

That's the truth, and in it lies the first problem:

Given that only violence can stop violence, and given that a modern, affluent, egalitarian society requires a certain amount of peace and trust to operate, who will be responsible for wielding this violence-stopping violence?

In caste systems throughout the world, there is a warrior caste with the power to make war externally and visit justice internally. In European history, the nobility of the medieval period were professional fighters responsible both for war abroad and for justice on their own lands.

There were problems inherent in this model. What we consider an "abuse of power" had no meaning to the medieval mind. The lord had the power and could use it as he saw fit. Only a more powerful lord could intervene and only as far as he felt the force available to him would carry the day.

Modern societies have been forced to work with both the *fact* that force is sometimes necessary and the social *belief* that force is inherently wrong—the "last resort of the ignorant." The modern solution has been to create professions, soldiers and police, authorized to use force in the name of and for the benefit of society as a whole.

Looked at shallowly, this seems to present a paradox. If a John Wayne Gacy or Jeffrey Dahmer (serial killers and rapists, and Dahmer a cannibal) handcuffs someone and takes them against their will to another place, it is kidnapping. When an officer does it, it is an arrest. When a citizen shoots another citizen, it is usually murder. When an officer shoots someone, it is closely scrutinized, but it is usually an 'incident,' not a crime.

The analogy doesn't hold true all the time. Most of the time, officers *are* expected to act like citizens—follow traffic laws, respect other people's property, and not randomly blaze away with their handguns.

But when law enforcement officers are being *enforcement* officers, it isn't a 'most of the time' situation. The standard social rules, the way that life and people are expected to be, have already failed or started the downhill slide. 'Most of the time' people respect each other's persons and property. 'Most of the time' people can be reasoned with and will do the right thing. 'Most of the time' you don't need the cops.

Referees in any sport are not and cannot be held to the same standards as players. They have to do things players aren't supposed to do, such as confront other players and sometimes eject them from the game.

When you do need officers to respond, it is because the social rules, the way most of us agree things *should be*, are being ignored.

Someone has decided to act the way he wants to instead of the way he should. It is unlikely that the social corrections will work when people are already off the social map.

About Me

That's the 'why' of the book. This is what I bring to the table:

For seventeen years, I was a corrections officer and sergeant working booking, maximum security, and mental health units. During that time, I trained corrections and enforcement officers* primarily in force-related skills, like defensive tactics (hand-to-hand fighting and arrest techniques) and force policy.

Working direct supervision corrections (and especially booking) exposes a young officer to a wide variety of 'difficult people.' I was told early in my career that two years in booking would result in more experience with hand-to-hand fighting than a career in enforcement. I don't know if that is true. I do know that I have instructed a group of enforcement officers with 180 years of cumulative experience and had more force incidents than all of them combined.

In the course of my duties, I spent more than a decade on the Tactical Team, much of that as the team leader. We were the ones who got called when no one else felt confident about handling the situation. I was trained (but did not serve) as a Hostage Negotiator. I was, for a time, the sergeant designated to handle problems with mentally ill inmates.

That much exposure was a powerful incentive to understand the rules of force as well as to investigate ways to avoid it.

I have also worked as an Internal Affairs investigator and as a contract advisor for the Iraqi federal corrections service.

About You

In an egalitarian society, the basic rules for *how much* force is legal are the same for officers as for civilians. The big differences come

* Corrections officers work inside the jails and prisons; enforcement officers make arrests and give tickets.

into play based on *when* and *how* force is used. A civilian who can walk away would not (should not, in most jurisdictions) use force, whereas an officer with a Duty to Act may have no choice. In cases of self-defense, citizens need to use force primarily to safely escape. Taking someone into custody requires different skills and entails different risks.

That will be covered in more detail later.

As much as possible I will put you inside the head of an officer—as a rookie at the academy in the first section, to growing into a veteran officer in the third. Every officer has been a civilian. Few civilians have ever been officers. Try it on for size.

The Format of This Book

This book is divided into two main sections with two smaller sections.

The first, "Training," shows what officers learn and how they are taught to think about Force. It will essentially be an introductory Use of Force class as it would be taught in many police academies. There will be some differences. Different jurisdictions have different policies. Another instructor might not emphasize what I do. What you will read in section one is almost exactly what you would experience if you were a rookie I was training.

Section two is a bridge. At the Academy, Use of Force is taught in a complicated web of other skills: gathering and preserving evidence, relevant law, driving, report writing, cross-cultural communication, etc.

You won't get that matrix of skills from a single book or even a dozen. There are a few things officers are taught that do pertain directly to force decisions and some things that will help you, as a civilian, put things in context. There will be an overview of how much time the officers spend on force skills, such as shooting and defensive tactics, at the academy.

Section two will also cover what happens when an officer is accused of breaking the rules. There will also be a short section on how self-defense law differs for civilians, in case you are interested.

The third section, "Experience," will describe how officers begin to see the world that they live in and how they feel about it.

It is artificial to separate training from experience, and there will be many places where I wish the human brain could read two things at once and blend and contrast them. There are some things taught in training (such as the difference between levels of force and levels of resistance) that often don't make sense, even to officers, until they come in contact with the real world. There are other issues, such as 'active shooter' tactics, where the doctrine flies in the face of experience.

Somewhere in the fog between training and experience, the officer has to make a decision. Sometimes the decision will be made in a fraction of a second on partial information. Sometimes the decision will change the lives of everyone involved forever.

The last section is a short piece about applying what you have read. It will probably hurt your feelings, since in much of it I will talk to you as if you were a suspect. Try to keep an open mind anyway. The easy part will cover what you should have learned. The hard parts will be about why community action fails and what can really be done—which is hard work and risk, not meetings and press conferences—and how you should behave when faced by an officer.

You are already a citizen and have your own experiences and points of view. In the bulk of the book, I will try to put you in the headspace of an officer to give you an overview of his training and a taste of his experience. In the very last section, I will try to let you feel like a suspect. That's a lot of mind-bending for one book. Get plenty of sleep and drink lots of water.

SECTION 1: TRAINING

I took my initial Use of Force training a very long time ago. There were a couple of hours of pre-service training when we were hired, some on-the-job training, and then the academy. We were given refresher training, usually one hour, at our annual in-service training after that.

Use of Force gets trained a lot because it is one of the "high-liability" subjects—the things that agencies commonly get sued over. It needs to be pounded into recruits and senior officers alike because high-speed judgments under stress are the meat of the job. Most of the rest of the things we do could be done by others—there's a lot of community service, helping stranded motorists, a lot of giving directions. Some counseling. Lots and lots of writing reports.

But the thing we do that others don't is face down angry, enraged, and often armed people. If the average person has trouble telling a salesman 'No,' he will have far more trouble telling an enraged meth addict swinging a chain 'No.' That's the job. And it's not enough to merely stop the bad guy. Most times anyone with a shotgun could stop anybody else. It is doing it in such a way that no one is offended, and that is hard because any use of force looks shocking to the uninitiated.

1.1 The Bottom Line

Everything that comes later will revolve around this concept. This is the basic tenet of using force for both civilians and officers:

You are expected and required to use the minimum level of force that you reasonably believe will safely resolve the situation.

Almost every word in that sentence is a legal concept.

A civilian is expected to use the minimum force—no more—that is necessary to resolve the situation. The officer, however, may be *required* to use that level of force. This hinges on the "Duty to Act," a concept that will be discussed at length in section 1.3.

The minimum level of force will be discussed in section 1.6, "The Force Continuum."

'Reasonably believe' can be very subjective, and there is a lot of case law trying to narrow it down. In any situation there is an almost infinite number of things that can happen: decisions that can be made, actions that can be taken. The reasonable person rule requires that whatever decision was made falls within the ballpark of what another reasonable person (ideally the jury members) might have done.

The rule is slightly different for Law Enforcement Officers (LEOs). The 'reasonable person' is exchanged for the 'reasonable officer' rule. The courts recognize that the difference in training and experience between an average reasonable citizen and an experienced officer can be vast. An officer who has been in a hundred fights will not see the situation the same way as a citizen who had one fight in junior high school, thirty years ago.

Further, courts and sensible people everywhere acknowledge that the officer can only be responsible for what he could have reasonably known at the time. He will never know if the three-hundred-pound man trying to take his gun has a heart condition, or that the drug dealer running from him is basically a nice person. He cannot fight differently or choose different ways to avoid fighting based on things he doesn't know.

Monday-morning quarterbacks and armchair generals are clichés in our society. The academic expert on application of force is no more credible.

Officers "are often required to make split-second judgments—in circumstances that are tense, uncertain, and rapidly evolving—about the amount of force that is necessary . . ."*

HARD TRUTH #4

Sometimes an officer will be forced to make a decision in a fraction of a second on partial information where the BEST choice will leave a corpse, a widow, two orphans, and someone who needs therapy.

* Graham v. Conner 490 U.S. 386 (1989).

Listen up, recruit—

You will make mistakes. A lot of them. You will have only the information you can gather in a few seconds and you will act on that partial information in a heartbeat. Almost every time, you will make the best decision you could have made. You will, however, be judged by people who have the leisure and resources to do research.

Where you saw a man acting angry, confused and ignoring your attempts to communicate, they will identify, perhaps, a deaf man who was despondent over a lost job or a family illness.

When he swung his fist at you and you had to decide what to do in a fraction of a second, the theorists will have hours or even days to think of a response that they believe would have worked 'better'—that is, more safely and more effectively. From their point of view, with these advantages in time and knowledge, almost every decision you make can be called a mistake.

You *will* make mistakes, by their standards and by your own standards as well. As your instructors, we will do what we can to make sure that you make these mistakes safely, in training.

Training is the place for mistakes.

Years ago, we designed and ran a "Confrontational Simulations" course. In a ConSim course, the goal is to present realistic, high-stress situations and force the student to make hard decisions under extreme pressure. The goal of this particular class was to bring Corrections Officers, who were accustomed to being unarmed in a relatively controlled environment, up to speed on decisions and survival skills when they were working fully armed and outside the jail.

> Many of the scenarios were intense: walking into armed robberies, former inmates wanting attention (good or bad), assassination attempts on high-profile offenders. Some were designed to draw a bad decision: in one case, exactly mimicking the assassination attempt, the 'threat' was a reporter with a microphone.
>
> One scenario was just an elderly lady crying on a park bench. The officers were good and compassionate people. Most who went through the scenario spent endless energy trying to engage her in conversation, or provide some sort of help. The goal of the

scenario was to remind the officers that not everything is their problem.

One of the officers, who shall remain nameless, asked and talked and even pled with the old woman. He finally ordered her to quit crying and tell him what was wrong. She continued to howl and sob. He repeated the order. She kept crying.

He pulled his pepper spray and hosed her down!

We ended the scenario. The officer then had to turn to a jury of his peers (the other officers taking the course) and justify his actions. He couldn't, of course. No reasonable officer would have done anything similar.

Neither would this officer, in real life. The situation was designed to ramp up his adrenaline. Even more, in the class setting he thought, with impeccable logic, that given a problem, his job was to find a solution. When everything else failed (and only when everything else failed), he tried force. It never occurred to him, in a classroom setting, that he was allowed to walk away, that not every situation is a situation requiring action.

You are expected and required to use the minimum level of force that you reasonably believe will safely resolve the situation.

'Safely' is very specific, and something hard for people raised on western movies and concepts of fair-play to grasp. I'll hit it again in section 1.2 on the "Three Golden Rules," but you deserve a taste here.

Real violence, real fighting, and real applications of force are not games. There is no reset button. There are no do-overs. A professional in this situation cannot afford some misguided idea of chivalry or fair play. Were the officer to indulge in that illusion, the bad guy would win half the time and go on to victimize more of the innocents the officer is sworn to protect.

At the swearing-in ceremony, when the Chief handed me my badge he said, "Once you pin this on, you are never allowed to lose. Never."

> The more force you use, the safer it is for you. Do the math. The threat* comes at you with no weapon, and you may try to wrestle with him and you might win. Or you may hit him upside the head and you may win. Or you could hit him with a club and you will probably win. Or you could pull a knife or gun and almost certainly win. The higher the level of force you use, the safer for you.
>
> The key is that you must judge the lowest level that will safely work. An experienced officer with decades in martial arts specialized in joint locks could handle many things, *safely*, at a lower level than other officers.
>
> * "Threat" is the standard law enforcement euphemism for anyone who makes the officer use force—the bad guy, in other words.

So, officer or civilian, you do not go into a situation at the level of force in which you believe you *might* prevail. You go into it as hard as you need to in order to go home safely.

'Safely,' as you see, modifies 'minimum level.' It is one short sentence, but it gets very complicated, especially in application.

Lastly, to 'resolve the situation' can mean something different in almost any encounter. The level of force needed to stop a man from kicking another man to death may be different from the level of force necessary to stop a sniper from pulling a trigger, and will definitely be different from the force needed to get handcuffs on a drunk and drive him to detox. The goals of a Use of Force (broadly to gain compliance or get control) are extremely variable, and that modifies everything.

> You are expected and required to use the minimum level of force that you reasonably believe will safely resolve the situation.

1.2 The Three Golden Rules

1. You and your partners go home safely at the end of each and every shift
2. The criminal goes to jail
3. Liability free

The three golden rules, first written by Dep. Paul McRedmond of the Multnomah County Sheriff's Office, must be the basis of all officer training. The fact that they exist, that they are explicitly taught, and that they needed to be stated so clearly says something about the profession.

Rule #1: You and your partners go home safely at the end of each and every shift

In most professions, staying alive and uninjured during the workday is more or less expected. Statistically, this is true for officers also. Most days, most go home fine. But some days, they don't. They are paid to sometimes deal with less-than-fully-socialized people in volatile situations. Officers are expected to walk (or run) into places where people with more common sense are running away.

Rule #1 is a pipe dream. The only safe way to do the job is to NOT do the job. Some officers *do* use this strategy and get away with it. We'll talk about Lops in "Experience," section three. The essence of Rule #1 is not to make the job any riskier than it is. Don't take stupid chances.

You might die, but you should never die because of your own stupidity or bravado. You should never get your partner killed because you couldn't keep your ego in check. And you should never, ever, die in such a way that other agencies use it for training films.

A short list of things to remember:

- You are not Superman and bullets do not bounce off you. This is one of the Hollywood Effects. By the time you join a police agency, you have watched thousands of hours of television. In the television world, being the good guy seems to magically protect you from serious injury. This isn't true. We all know it isn't true, but seeing it a thousand times can hit the brain at a very deep level and rookies often act like it is true.

- Keep your ego in check. This is a job, not an identity. Criminals will try to bait you, or try to make you angry. If you lose control, they can manipulate the situation. It is your job to manipulate the situation. You have to do everything in your power to stay above the game, so that you can see and think clearly.
- Never take it (almost anything) personally. You are going to be interacting with people on their worst days. They will be angry, frightened, and indignant. It's not about you. If someone needs to get his sense of masculinity back by calling you names, stay cool. It's better than if he gets it back by beating his wife or children, which might be his normal method.
- Don't get too excited to watch your back. This is a hard one to teach and a hard one to do. When the adrenaline hits, you will get tunnel vision and physically be unable to see things in your peripheral vision. Another factor is that attention is naturally drawn to the point of action or the greatest perceived threat. You will want to look at what is going on. Sometimes it will be your job to make sure no one comes up from behind. Even if it isn't, make a conscious decision to look around and see if the situation has changed.
- Do not compete with criminals. You do not have to show that you are more manly than a wife beater. You do not have to be more clever than a con man.
- You are not alone. Long nights on solo patrol it is easy to forget that you are part of a team. You have a radio, use it.
- More than that, not just in the day-to-day stuff but also in a serious crisis, *you are not alone*. Your agency has decades or centuries of experience to draw from. Never be afraid to ask for advice or guidance, or just tips on how to do a better job.
- You have a radio for a reason. That ties into the above. Just add—don't get lazy. Call in every stop. Just because the last three hundred stops went fine is no indication that the next one will. Someone needs to know where you are and what you are doing. You will use the radio far more than you will use any weapon or force option. Get good at it.
- It is not a game. There is no ref, no time limit, and the stakes are higher than any game. Do not go into this thinking in contest terms. The job gets done. There is no "I'll be the best cop I can,

and he'll be the best crook he can, and we'll see who wins." There is no 'see who wins.' You get the job done. You are not permitted to lose or draw. You have a responsibility to the citizens.

- You don't need to prove your masculinity. I think I've said this three different ways now. Sinking in?

You have a responsibility to keep yourself safe. You have a job to do and you cannot do it if you are dead or injured. A dead officer is not just a heroic or tragic icon, a dead officer is also a wasted resource.

The most succinctly I have ever heard this concept explained was at Combat Medic training at Fort Sam Houston. The instructors drilled a simple truth into our heads: A dead medic never saved anybody. This simple truth is just as true for officers.

An officer who gets himself killed or seriously injured becomes part of the problem. He can't help anyone else. He can't save the damsel in distress. Worse, the people needed to save the damsel now need to allocate resources to saving the stupid guy too.

When an officer gets killed in the line of duty training units and individual officers all over the country will try to find out what happened in as much detail as possible. Hoping to find out where the officer made a mistake. Mistakes can be fixed. Bad luck can't.

> Long ago, an officer and friend sent a message out into cyberspace. A friend of his had been killed. The friend was a good officer: fit, alert, well-trained, good judgment. Everything you would want in an officer and a partner. He had come around a corner and been shot in the face. Game over.

When an officer dies, we always hope it was a mistake, because we might be able to protect ourselves and our rookies from a mistake. Getting our heads blown off coming around a corner . . . not much you can do.

The Immutable Order was originally codified for hostage rescue. It is a cold and logical assessment of who is more important—the officer, the hostage, the bystanders, or the threat. It is not about love or duty or nobility, but simply a cold look at goals and resources.

The operator (officer)'s safety comes first because the officer is needed to save the hostages. If the officer becomes a casualty, not only is he out of the equation but also every other operator, accessory, and piece of equipment needed to save *him* cannot help to save the hostages.

Second come the hostages. They are the reason for being there.

Third come the bystanders and civilians. Yes, they are important. Yes, they shouldn't be hurt . . . but they also shouldn't be there at all. They should be safely away. Unlike the hostages, the bystanders have a choice and have some responsibility if stray bullets or collapsing buildings come their way.

Lastly are the hostage takers. All life is precious and all that, but the bad guys (BG) created the situation. The primary job is making sure that no citizen dies for the BG's anger, greed, or stupidity. If the only way to ensure that is with the death of the bad guy . . . sorry, pal. You should have made a different choice.

Putting the officer first seems cold and it is—but do the math.

The "Immutable Order" is not a statement of value. It is not saying that the life of the officer is more *valuable* than the lives of the hostages. It is the way the resources, goals, and obstacles must be prioritized in order to get the job done. If an officer in a hot patrol area really valued his own life over even random strangers, he wouldn't be in this business.

At the Columbine School shooting, the first responding officers started to go in and were called back by cooler-headed administrators. They were told to do what policy said: Set up a perimeter and wait for the SWAT team. More children died while they waited.

There was a huge outcry from citizens, the media, politicians, and even the officers themselves. Doctrine was changed, and, almost nationwide, the current standard for an active shooter scenario is to go in, immediately, with the first four officers on the scene. (This is changing too, and some agencies are experimenting with going in with the first officer or first pair on the scene.)

Everyone involved felt like they were doing the right thing: The first officers followed their instincts—very little hits you harder at a gut level than someone killing kids. The administrators who called them back were doing what they had trained, and what they had been taught was the best solution. The citizens and politicians and media were rightly outraged, and demanded change, and they got it.

But I have trained this scenario a lot—usually playing the bad guy. Every time, EVERY TIME, all of the responding officers die,* and I am free to go back to shooting kids. But it's policy now, and that makes it officially the right thing to do.

This example isn't about politics, or who is right, or who is wrong. It is about something you will see every day on the job—screwed-up situations where every last person involved is trying to do the right thing. I've trained the scenario. I know the officers die. But in my heart, I'm with the first group of officers who went in anyway.

Rule #2: The criminal goes to jail

This isn't worded the same for all branches of law enforcement. For Corrections, the criminal stays in jail. For Parole and Probation, you try to prevent the criminal victimizing more people. For bailiffs, you keep the courtroom under control.

The essence is that you have a job to do. Do the job. Sometimes it's hard and sometimes it's boring and sometimes it's terrifying and sometimes you don't care. Tough. Do the job.

This is an easy job to burnout on. You see the worst of humanity at its worst. People lie to you. Even people who are good people get a little nervous when talking to cops and they try to make themselves sound better. It's human nature to distrust and even dislike people who lie to you.

Dealing with the victims will hit you harder than dealing with

* Sort of. One of the rules with simulation training is that the officer continues no matter how many times he has been shot so that they are mentally programmed to "win." They always get the bad guy in the end. But Sims are marking rounds and in every scenario I've done, all of the officers had marks on the helmet, groin protectors, and other vital unarmored places. To be fair, a friend of mine, an elite officer in his agency, tends to win in these scenarios, but he's pretty extraordinary.

the predators. Sometimes a predator is so cold as to seem alien. He or she can shake your assumptions about what it means to be human. You will meet predators who do not distinguish between a mate, a child, and a toy: They are all just possessions to be used. It will bother you, but it doesn't hurt. Dealing with the victims, with the tears and blood, will hurt. Sometimes, it will seem easier to quit paying attention, to quit caring.

Rule #2 is simple. (Don't forget that Rule #1 is the prerequisite—If you are injured or dead, you can't do the job.) Do the job. Do it well. Do it like a professional. Not like a crusader. Definitely not like a self-righteous, angry prick. No matter how you feel, do a professional job. You get more convictions that way.

These concepts have to be hammered into new recruits hard and are an integral part of training. Most rookies come to the job with a hero complex. They want to save the world. They want to make a difference.

That's great. One of the big goals of training is to preserve these dreams but implant the practical skills necessary to make the dreams work.

HARD TRUTH #5

You can't achieve a dream by dreaming.

Training will never be quite right. It will never be enough—not enough to ensure that all the rookies will make good decisions or even that all the rookies will survive. All of us come to the job with assumptions built into the image of *doing the right thing*. We think that if we save a life, it will be a good person or an innocent child, and they will be grateful, and the world will be a better, safer place. We aren't ready for saving a bum from drowning, and having him complain because we let him get wet. We aren't prepared for the day we actually stop a rape in progress, and the rapist sues because his neck or elbow hurt afterwards.

Once in a great while, you will hear, "Thank you."

This is the real secret: The people who do this job well for a long time don't do it for the rewards or the recognition. They don't do it (after the first year or two) for the rush. They don't even do it to make the world a better place.

They do it because they can and most people can't. Every shattered body they see, every terrifying brawl in the dark, and every interminable wait for blood tests to see if they have been exposed to a disease that might change or end their lives, are experiences that no one else needs to have.

Rookies need to learn to do the job, and do it like a professional, not like a TV hero. That way lies madness.

Rule #3: Liability free

Litigation is a hallmark of modern society. From their earliest training, officers are taught to fear lawsuits. They are taught that anything they do can be twisted in court, and cost them their house, their savings, and their retirement.

In reality, that is rarely the case. As long as the officer stays within his or her agency policy and law, any liability stays with that agency. Reality doesn't make the fear any less real. In the excellent book, *Deadly Force Encounters,* Alexis Arwohl and Loren Christensen point out that in actual shootings, with bullets flying at them and their lives in imminent peril, officers were almost universally plagued with the thought, "I'm gonna get sued." That's not a thought you can afford when your life is on the line.

There has been a sea change since I started in this profession. Years ago, there was a presumption that the officers were the good guys and the criminal was the bad guy. It seems to a lot of officers that this has changed.

One of the ways it has affected the job is in how reports were written. When I started this job, I was specifically told that when we used force, the reports were to be as minimal as possible. I was told, "What you don't put in, they can't use against you." "They," of course, were civil litigation attorneys, internal affairs . . . anyone who might have a reason to scrutinize what you did. We also were often told to write reports only on incidents that were likely to result in scrutiny—"No blood, no foul."

It was wrong and must have made it much easier to cover abuses when they did happen . . . but thinking had already begun to change. Attorneys are smart and they fully understand that there are lies of omission as well as commission. Now, the reports are expected to be excruciatingly thorough, to cover everything you did and everything you saw. It was a big change, but it resulted in an important lesson.

The key to Rule #3, to being successful in litigation, or prevent litigation altogether is to make good decisions, to carry them out properly, and then to write a damn good report. Failure at any one of these three steps can really hurt you.

Making good decisions has two different meanings. Most officers, most of the time, make good decisions because they are good people. That holds true for anyone. When a decision must be made in a split second that decision will be based on *who you are*. Somewhere in the balance of fear and internal ethics, the person will make a decision (or fail to make a decision). Good, ethical people make good, ethical decisions.

Good decision-making is also a product of training, experience, and good policy. As much as officers need to be taught how to drive in an emergency, how to shoot, how to preserve evidence, and a thousand other things, they also have to be taught how to think, how to prioritize what they see, and how to make decisions. This will all be refined and expanded with experience.

Good policy is critical as well. One private company that regularly deals with violent mentally ill people has decided that they can't be sued for hugging. The company has made it policy that the only self-defense technique allowed is to hug the attacker until he or she calms down. The environment is not designed for security and the clients have access to a number of things that can be altered to become weapons. Hugging someone trying to stab you is one of the less effective options. A bad policy, and this is a very bad policy, can put the employee in the position of following the rules or dying.

Carrying out your decisions properly is a matter of training. Knowing what to do is not the same as knowing how to do it. As an example, an agency that allows punching in their force continuum must train the officers in how to punch, or they will be sending officers to the hospital with broken hands. That violates the first golden rule.

Then, whatever your decision and action, you must *write it well.* You must be able to explain to your peers, superiors, and, if necessary, a jury exactly what you did; why you did it; and why it was the best option. Federal Air Marshall Guthrie says, "Your report can't make a bad shoot good, but it can make a good shoot bad."

No matter how much you twist or massage the words of your report, you can't turn a bad decision into a good decision. Maybe you can fool some people, but it is still a bad decision. Like polishing a turd, it still stinks.

A bad report *can* sink you. Doing the right thing for the wrong reason can change a heroic act to a crime. "He was going to hit the baby with the hammer so I shot him," is justified. "He was an ass, so I shot him," is homicide.

Using a higher level of force might require explaining why a lower level of force would not have worked: "I was too far away to tackle the suspect before he hit the baby with the hammer. I had no choice but to fire my weapon."

Make a good decision. Execute it properly. Write a good report.

The Three Golden Rules

1. You and your partners go home safely at the end of each and every shift
2. The criminal goes to jail
3. Liability free

1.3 The Duty to Act

Let's say you, as a citizen, see someone in your front yard, acting strangely, staring and shouting and singing songs about John Lennon and Satan. Instead of calling 911, you go out on your front porch and yell, "Hey! What are you doing? Get out of my yard!" The Emotionally Disturbed Person (EDP) takes off and runs.

As a citizen, you've solved the problem. He may be in somebody else's yard, but he's not in yours. You aren't responsible for him or for his actions.

As an officer, you have a duty to act. This can be really specific or really vague, depending on the policies of an individual agency and current tactical training. Once an issue comes to the officer's attention, the officer is not only responsible for what he does, but for what happens if he chooses to do nothing.

Crazy guy runs and leaves a citizen's yard because the citizen yelled. Fine. Crazy guy then slaughters a few people at the neighbor's house: No liability or responsibility to the citizen.

The officer has to think of consequences—crazy, running guy might launch himself in front of a bus. Or hurt someone else. Or be wanted for a previous crime. Or desperately need psychiatric meds.

This is just an example, but the officer will respond to clues inherent in the scenario. Most people don't run at the approach of an officer, hence it's reasonable to believe that if someone runs, there is a reason. The subject might have a mental stability issue, in which case the officer may need to get medical help. Or the runner may have a warrant out for his arrest (no one wants to be the officer/agency who let a wanted felon go because they didn't take the time to check for warrants). It may be because he has weapons or drugs on him that he is afraid they will find . . .

So the officer chases, and it is reasonable. Furthermore, if he wants to do the job, he has no choice. Many of the disconnects between police and citizen perceptions of force incidents center here. The citizen asks if the force was really necessary.

For a citizen, it *wouldn't* have been necessary. Citizens aren't required or expected to rush toward danger. Citizens are not responsible for the safety of the people around them and citizens, usually, can't be censured or disciplined if they fail to stop someone else's bad acts.

If a man with a knife runs toward an occupied house, the citizen has no responsibility to the people inside. An officer does and may need to make a choice to shoot a man in the back and live with the consequences of that choice . . . or to *not* shoot him and live with the possibility that the threat might kill children in the house.

> There are no perfect answers in most tense situations. There are few, if any solutions where all parties involved are going to walk away with a smile in their hearts. Sometimes there aren't even good answers. Sometimes there will be orphans. The officer's duty in those situations is to try to choose the least bad answer.
>
> To call a decision 'bad' we must have an alternate answer that we are sure would have resulted in less tragedy.

This is not a choice that a citizen is likely ever to make. It is one that officers have made. And they have had to live with the consequences. It is nothing short of choosing between nightmares—you will either live with the consequences of your actions or the consequences of your inaction. You will never know if the other choice would have been better or worse.

Not every police decision involves life or death. The officer needs skills that cover everything from mediation and calming down enraged EDPs to hand-to-hand skills, hand weapons, chemical sprays, and firearms.

Because of the *duty to act*, officers need skills that rarely enter into civilian self-defense. The things that can be handled with a wristlock or an escort hold are also the situations that a citizen can likely avoid.

Not only do officers need high-end self-defense skills and are more likely to use these skills than most civilians, they need an entirely separate set of skills for defending a third party or breaking up a fight.

Duty to act not only puts more moral pressure on the officer, exposing him or her to ugly, no-win situations, but also increases the complexity of those possible situations. It requires a broader base of skills than are needed by people who can choose to simply leave.

Duty to Act When You Can't Do Anything

Sometimes, there is nothing the officer can do. Or nothing he or she can safely do. Or there is a good chance immediate intervention without proper training, equipment, and support will make matters worse. In cases like these, the duty to act can be satisfied by getting to a safe place, keeping an eye on the threat, and calling for help.

Very few officers are trained in hostage negotiations, for instance. When a lone officer stumbles into something that either is or becomes a hostage situation, it is safer for everyone, in most cases, for the officer to pull back and call the specialists. Amateur hostage negotiators can make matters worse. Storming a barricaded subject, with or without hostages, is a dangerous specialty. Individuals being heroic can quickly become hostages themselves.

At the heart of these kinds of decisions is "officer discretion." Every situation is different, as is every officer and every threat. Officers must cultivate the judgment and be empowered to make the decisions when they are presented with a situation.

This is inherently risky and one of those factors that can make citizens very uncomfortable. It makes officers uncomfortable, too. Officers are rarely required to make an arrest or issue a citation in misdemeanor cases. It varies by policy, but in most places, if an officer happens to see a six-year-old shoplift a candy bar, the officer can tell the kid to give it back and apologize.

That discretion—to give the kid guidance or start a juvenile record and get a bunch of agencies involved—is a huge power. It is both feared and necessary. Too often, it also feels like a trap, a trap with no right answers.

On the feared side, turning a blind eye is also a form of discretion. An officer can avoid confrontation just by not doing the job. Discretion to let a minor lawbreaker go could be based less on whether the message was sent (the verbal warning for a traffic infraction) than on who it was—friend, family, another officer. Discretion is also the crack that people of power try to pry at: "Do you know who my father is? Can't we just make this go away?"

Fear can be rationalized as discretion. Stopping a high-speed chase or not engaging in a Use of Force or not chasing a running suspect can all easily be rationalized—they can be dangerous, and sometimes the danger to the threat, yourself, and bystanders, isn't justified by the potential result. What level of force would you be willing use for a city noise ordinance? For a car theft, are you willing to risk tearing through a school zone at lunchtime at 90 mph? There are good and bad reasons for making any of these decisions.

At the extreme, discretion can become abuse of authority. The "reasonable officer" rule is vague. It has to be, because the situations in which you need it are impossible to script. In that vagueness, it is possible for a bad or fearful officer to perceive justifications for things he wants, not needs, to do.

There is no easy answer for this one, no line that can be drawn that will make everyone happy. We all want 'justice' but that is a hard concept to define. If 'justice' were based simply on results, motivation wouldn't matter and there would be no difference between intentional murder and accidental manslaughter. Justice-as-retribution collides with the concept of 'behavior modification.'

> Once upon a time I was driving a marked patrol car* and passed a car with a young couple in it. The wife was in the passenger seat with a toddler on her lap. Big no-no in my state with a very hefty fine. I passed, made eye contact with the driver, got a ways ahead and pulled over. The couple stopped their car and put the baby in the child seat. They drove on past, and I waved.

In a world with no officer discretion (and a jurisdiction where Corrections Officers had arrest powers), I might have been *required* to pull them over and write a ticket. There was nothing about their car to indicate that they had money to burn on fines or court fees. The kid was safe. What more did I want?

There are some areas and some laws where discretion has been outlawed—'will arrest' rules. For instance, if someone calls in a domestic violence complaint in many jurisdictions, *someone* has to go to jail, at least for the night or until bail is posted. Officers have made mistakes in judgment that had tragic results, most famously when

* Full disclosure—I was a Corrections Sergeant and didn't have any authority or business enforcing traffic laws, but since it was a marked car and I was in uniform, no one else knew that. Whenever we were on the road, there was a potential that the office would receive a complaint because we 'ignored' a traffic violation.

Konerak Sinthasomphone briefly escaped from Jeffrey Dahmer. Officers responding to a naked, dazed, and raped fourteen-year old boy decided it was a 'lover's spat,' and returned the boy to the serial killer cannibal, who did what serial killer cannibals do.

So, removing discretion in this case is good, right? Sort of. Except bad people have an amazing ability to use good things for bad ends. The 'will arrest' rule has become a harassment tool in divorce cases, and a way to empty a house for burglary while one spouse is in jail and the other is trying to arrange bail. It is one of the few issues where no evidence is needed for an arrest. The expectation is that there will be no serious repercussions unless found guilty at trial, so no harm, no foul. In theory.

But what if you have a job where you can be fired for missing a day? What if a day in jail causes you to miss a mandatory custody hearing? A lot of well-meant legislation can have unintended consequences.

1.4 The Goal

Force is a form of communication, the most emphatic possible way of saying, "No!" or "Stop that!" or "Do it now!"

An officer enters any use of force with a goal in mind: to get the handcuffs on; to remove the drunk from the premises or the car; to get out of the ambush alive. The preferred goal is always cooperation, where the citizen wants to do what the officer has already determined is necessary. You usually get this from citizens (citizens being slang for normal, good people):

Officer: Sir, please move to the other side of the street.
Citizen: Oh, of course. (Sometimes they even say, "thanks!")

If you can't get cooperation, an officer will settle for compliance where the citizen (or threat) may not be happy about it, but does what he or she needs to do:

Officer: Mr. Smith, we have a warrant for your arrest. I have to take you into custody.

Mr. Smith: This is fucking bullshit! I took care of that warrant a month ago!
Officer: Possibly, but I have to take you in. Will you turn around and put your hands behind your back?
Mr. Smith (turning around and putting hands behind his back)**:** Fuck you. I hope this makes you feel like a big man you fucking punk.

Mr. Smith is not happy, but he is compliant. In section three, "Experience," we'll talk more about criminals and the criminal subculture. Certain criminals will always be verbally abusive with officers. For some it is part of their identity; others know that verbal resistance combined with physical compliance is safe—the officer won't hurt him but his peers will see him as a tough guy. So many, many arrestees will act like Mr. Smith. But so will many citizens.

For some ordinary citizens, contact with the police will be associated with very bad events, such as being a victim of a crime. For many it will be the unpleasantness of a traffic ticket. Basically, even ordinary citizens usually come into contact with police on a bad day. That can

For both officer safety reasons and legal "fair and equal treatment" reasons, all fresh bookings into jail are treated the same. Murderer or drunk driver, we treat them exactly the same because, truth to tell, just because someone got arrested for Driving Under the Influence of Intoxicants (DUII) doesn't mean that he doesn't have a bunch of bodies buried in his crawl space.

We take everyone's shoe laces because some people attempt suicide with them. We search everyone thoroughly because some people try to get weapons and drugs into the housing units. We take off wedding rings because you may be housed in an area where someone is willing to bite your finger off for something shiny.

Consistently, in booking, some of the worst fights we have are with first-time offenders who feel that they aren't "real criminals" and should be dealt with differently. They stand up for rights that not only do they not have, but for rights that we are prohibited by policy to extend.

influence the citizen to act in ways that they would normally never consider.

This is often compounded by the officer's indifference. I almost wrote "seeming indifference" but in many of the day-to-day calls, the indifference is real: going to jail may be the most traumatic experience of your life, but I've booked, as a corrections officer, over sixty arrests in one night. I won't be as excited as you are, I guarantee it.

If neither cooperation nor compliance is an option, the officer must take control. This is sometimes referred to as 'forcing compliance' but I am trying to keep the language clear.

Most of this book is about the nuances of how an officer gains control. *'The least force necessary to . . .'* In general, control is considered established when the threat is handcuffed or placed in a cell—*restrained* or *contained*, respectively. Restraints limit the threat's means; containment limits his opportunity.

Force is never to be used for punishment. Legally and ethically, the duty of an officer is to bring the threat to the justice system for his guilt to be determined and for the courts to set punishment. Punishment is not the officer's job.

There is another, deeper reason that experienced officers come to understand—a very practical reason why force is never to be used as punishment completely separate from theories of justice or ethics. We will discuss that insight in section 1.9, "Scaling Force."

1.5 The Threat

Force is always used on a person and that person is called the Threat. There are several good reasons for that word. First and foremost, it is a reminder that it is the person's actions and capabilities that justify force. Not appearance, not smell, not history (though history can enter the equation). The Threat's ability to harm, to escape, sometimes just to sit there, is what justifies force.

In order to be an "immediate threat" the Threat must have Intent, Means, and Opportunity. And, the officer must be able to explain how he knew it.

Intent simply means that the Threat wanted to do something bad.

> Just as a homeowner can order you to leave his house, a business owner or event organizer can ask the police to order you to leave. In most jurisdictions, you must comply when an officer asks for ID. When Immigration asks to see your passport, you do not have the right to refuse. These are all lawful orders.
>
> A citizen does not have any right to refuse a lawful order. Officers can and, in some cases, will be required to use force to ensure the order is followed.

Pointing a gun indicates Intent. Yelling, "I'm gonna kill that bitch!" indicates Intent. Balling up a fist indicates Intent. Going limp or just sitting when ordered to leave indicates Intent.

Intent for what? To harm someone, including the officer, or a third party or for the threat to harm him- or herself. Or to break any law. Or to disobey a lawful order.

The Threat must also have Means. The officer needs to be able to explain why he reasonably believed that the Threat had what he needed to carry out his Intent. If a ninety-year-old woman struggling with a walker snarls, "I'm gonna tear your head off and shit down your neck," the words indicate some pretty serious Intent, but she probably lacks the Means. Tearing off a head is pretty difficult.

The third piece is Opportunity. The Threat must be able to reach you with the Means. If someone who has a gun and hates your guts is on another continent, he can't reach you. You can't justify nuking him. This comes up quite often in jail, where a threat in a cell screams threats at the officers. Locked in a cell, he lacks Opportunity and can't be treated as an immediate threat—and it is unprofessional to open the cell and give him the Opportunity.

In the officer's arsenal, handcuffs are meant to eliminate or limit Means; cells limit Opportunity.

What the officer sees, the Intent, Means, and Opportunity inherent in a specific threat at a specific time, establishes a *level of resistance*. The level of resistance is the primary factor in the officer's decision of what level of force to use.

In order to be compliant, a person must actually comply. If an officer lawfully orders someone to leave the premises and the person does not, the person is NOT complying. Even if he says, "Just a minute." Even if he yells, "Don't touch me. I am complying!" Actions matter, not words. Failure to comply *is* static resistance.

We had an arrestee down and he was biting, kicking, and trying to punch and scratch. The whole time he was yelling, "I'm not resisting! Police brutality!" One of the witnesses (fortunately only one) completely disregarded what she saw and reported what she heard.

Levels of Force

Levels of force and levels of resistance have different names in different agencies. Don't get hung up on names.

Levels of resistance are scaled as *None*, *Verbal*, *Static*, *Active*, *Ominous*, and *Lethal*.

None. A person not breaking any laws, not harming any person or thing and obeying any instructions from the officers is showing *no resistance*. No force, therefore, is necessary to stop the person from doing something bad or to make the person do something necessary. The person is compliant, even cooperative.

Verbal. In an incident of verbal resistance, the threat is doing what he needs to do—desisting from harm or obeying an order—but is being verbally abusive about it. It is common for low-level criminals to attempt to save face by threatening or insulting the officers. Most are experienced at getting arrested; they know our policy and can act tough with nearly complete confidence in their safety.

Some threats hope for a lawsuit in their favor. A desire for publicity will lead some to attempt to provoke officers into an unjustified use of force.

A local photographer told me she had attended classes run by a protest group specifically on how to bait officers into making a motion that would look like a strike on camera. For example, one protester would pretend to fling a cup of liquid at the officer.

> The cup would be empty, but when the officer's hand flinched up to protect his face, a photographer would be waiting at an angle such that the motion would look like a strike.

In general, force is not justified against a threat only exhibiting verbal resistance. This is not true in a correctional setting. In jails and prisons, the staff is routinely outnumbered by dozens and sometimes more than a hundred to one. The laws have recognized that under these conditions and with the necessity to maintain order in a population that is far more violent than the norm, the staff cannot safely allow anyone to incite others. Verbal resistance in a correctional institution, especially when viewed as an attempt to incite other inmates to action or show or gain leadership status with the inmates can and usually will be met with force.

Static. A threat refusing to comply with lawful orders, even if doing no harm, is exhibiting static resistance. Static resistance authorizes pain-compliance techniques. (See section 1.6, "The Force Continuum.")

As much as the average person has a problem with force at all, most can get behind the idea of using force to stop force. Using force to stop nothing is a little harder to accept.

Here's the rationale:

American or not, you don't have the right to do anything you want. Your rights stop where they interfere with another person's rights. People cannot take your things without permission. They cannot use your things without permission. Also, they cannot prevent you from using your things or prevent your lawful use of public things. Neither can you. Rights work in both directions.

Protesters who block traffic are infringing on the rights of every other citizen to use the road. Loud, angry people using foul language are infringing on everyone else's right to be in that place in peace. The politically impassioned heckler who decides that his insults and questions for a candidate are more important than the agenda is infringing on everyone else's rights.

Note well: In almost all cases an officer can't or won't intervene until he has been asked. In a private place, such as a business or rented

> Officers are sometimes forced to make decisions with incredible speed. They are often high-stakes decisions with a glance's worth of data. Is the threat pulling away to run or pulling away to hit me? That question takes me just under two seconds to say aloud. In that space of time, a completely untrained person could hit you eight times. I have several friends who could draw a knife and stab you eight times in under two seconds.
>
> Those are high-stakes decisions. Imagine dropping a piece of toast. Before it hits the ground, you have to decide if it will land with the butter side up or down, and you must do something before it hits . . . and the action you should take is based on which way it will hit.
>
> Same speed, same amount of information. The stakes are just higher—take a chance on being injured or take a chance on hurting someone who just may be a scared kid trying to get away.
>
> This is the standard that officers are often held to by the media and some civilians. It is beyond human ability in speed and analysis.

lecture hall, the request must come from someone with site authority, such as the owner or manager.

In order to protect the rights of others, officers are authorized and sometimes *required* to use force.

Active resistance is whenever the threat uses physical force to prevent the officer from doing the job. Running away is active resistance. Hanging on to a door jamb or a steering wheel to prevent being taken into custody is active resistance. Pulling away as an officer tries to apply handcuffs is active resistance; however, pulling away is also exactly what a threat who has decided to attack the officer might do and is often met with an appropriately higher level of force.

An *ominous* threat is trying to injure you, pure and simple. That can be any unarmed attack and some attacks with weapons (though most weapon attacks are *lethal*). Biting, also, is termed ominous behavior, although with concerns about blood-borne pathogens, some officers argue that biting should be considered lethal resistance.

Lethal threats, of course, are trying to kill you. Mechanism makes

> An officer's intent in a deadly force situation is not and can never be "to kill." The intent is always to 'stop the threat.' This can appear to be mincing words. In a way, it is. Killing is certainly stopping, and many of the ways a threat is 'stopped' that come to media attention are kills.
>
> There are two reasons why that wording is important in application and training. 'Dead' is a term with very specific meanings—something that is sometimes difficult to establish in the field. Modern medicine has saved many people who would have been declared dead fifty years ago. A 'reasonable officer' can be expected to determine when a threat has stopped; he cannot be expected to determine 'dead,' and that simple change in wording might require the officer to use *more* force, just to be sure that he met the standard.
>
> The second reason is for the benefit of the officer in the aftermath. This will be covered more in section three, but for now know that there is a cost, sometimes a terrible cost, in the taking of a human life. No matter how brutal the person or under what circumstances, converting someone from living to dead is not something the normal person can do without grave psychological repercussions. Reminding someone that they needed to stop the threat, that his or her intent was to make the threat stop, not to kill, may, in some tiny way, ease the healing process. Or so we hope.

no difference: kicking a person in the head when he is down, shooting, stabbing, throwing someone off a building or into traffic.

A lethal threat authorizes deadly force.

Often, even if the threat's intent is manifestly not lethal, but his or her actions place someone in mortal danger, the officer may use deadly force. In this context, think of force not as force intended to kill, but as doing anything it takes to stay alive. A threat struggling to escape on a narrow, slippery fire escape several stories off the ground, a threat trying to drive away from a traffic stop with the officer stuck halfway through the window, or a developmentally disabled 300-pound man struggling to escape from a small room and crushing the officer may all justify deadly force.

1.6 The Force Continuum

The basic concept of the force continuum is that different types of threats can be handled with different tactics. Not everything can be solved with a kind word or a wristlock and not every situation requires a gun. The force continuum is an attempt to scale needs to actions so that administrators, juries, and other interested parties can estimate whether the force used in a situation was appropriate.

The simple fact is that fights, especially some of the ugly ones that last a long time or involve extreme levels of force, are extremely chaotic and don't fit easily into boxes. Built into Use of Force training, along with all the levels of the force continuum, are all the reasons to depart from it.

As I write this, there is a debate raging in many agencies about whether to abandon the concept of a force continuum altogether. The argument for maintaining it is mentioned above: it makes certain elements of force application and policy easy to explain and to teach.

The arguments against are more varied. The most common complaint I hear from officers and trainers is that some officers and many juries will be led to believe that since the continuum is presented in steps, the officer is required to try every level, starting at the bottom, in every situation.

The attitude seems to be that if it is written into policy as a continuum, the format alone could influence citizens to believe that the officer is required to tap an armed hostage taker on the shoulder, and then attempt a takedown or wristlock, and then try a baton before shooting to save the hostage.

I have never actually seen someone who believed this, just heard rumors.

Another argument stems from the legal world. Graham v. Connor, 490 U.S. 386 (1989) is one of the fundamental findings that define force law and policy in the United States. One of the most far-reaching and important implications in Graham is the understanding that force incidents are so chaotic and unpredictable that it will never be possible to decide in advance, or to present a formula about what is and isn't appropriate.

In that hierarchy of preferences, there are a few that civilians express concern over that make sense to officers. The first is tangible harm versus emotional harm.

Certain segments of our society honestly believe that "words can cut like a knife." No one could believe that who had ever seen a knife wound. In order to accomplish a legitimate goal I will, if necessary, scream, insult or even demean rather than touch. I would rather, by far, hurt someone's feelings than someone's body. It is a lower level of force. It is preferable to be rude and have the offensive drunk leave on his own power than to be nice and push him out. Nice and no touch combined are better of course, but only if it works.

The second is the difference between injury and pain. Finger locks hurt. OC (pepper spray) hurts. Tasers hurt a lot. The injuries from these are minimal. Loud screams of pain bother people, and they should, but they are qualitatively different from the wet pop of a ligament tearing or the sickening thump of a head hitting concrete.

Some consider the continuum to be an attempt to write a cookie-cutter answer to a chaotic problem, explicitly against the guidance in Graham.

The most compelling argument, to my mind, is that with proper training, the continuum may not be necessary. The bottom line: *You are expected and required to use the minimum level of force that you reasonably believe will safely resolve the situation* plus understanding the "Factors and Circumstances" of section 1.7 gets to the same place.

I will be describing a continuum here. As a friend once said, "Models are models. Many are useful. None are true."

The reason is that models make some very important things easy to teach. They are common sense, but sometimes common sense needs a little explanation:

The officer doing absolutely nothing is the preferred use of force: people doing the right thing because it is the right thing and they are good people.

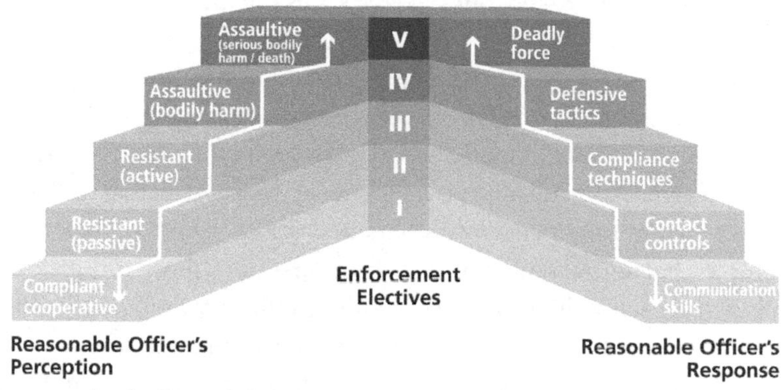

An example of a Force Continuum.

If that fails, the next best option is a gentle reminder, probably just a look.

If there must be interaction, it is better to engage reason than to hurt feelings, better to hurt feelings than to touch, better to touch than to hurt, better to hurt than to injure, and better to injure than to kill.

The force continua are just ways to put that order of preference into words.

What follows is just an example. Different agencies use different Force Continua and not all include the same things at the same levels. For instance, using pressure on the sides of the neck to cut off blood to the brain is considered by some agencies to be deadly force and by others to be a control technique.

The Levels of the Force Continuum

Level 1: Presence

An officer has a reasonable expectation that when he shows up at the scene people will stop misbehaving. This works in most instances. A cop car in your rear-view mirror is one of the more effective traffic control devices. Most normal people do not break laws in front of uniformed officers.

Officers are taught early in their careers that a professional appearance enhances their presence. It is easier to disrespect or ignore a slob than someone who looks like he takes the job, and therefore his duties, seriously.

Presence is a very powerful but very subjective attribute. In *On Killing*, Lt. Colonel David Grossman pointed out that even major military battles are won more often by display than by a physical destruction of the enemy. An impressive show of force—whether a line of musket men in bright coats with hats that make them look seven feet tall or a phalanx marching in perfect order—does more to break the will of the enemy than to increase killing efficiency, especially when combined with the confusion, smoke, and dust of real battle.

Officers use these concepts as well—lights and sirens, the black armor of the riot squad, and even the starched uniform, peaked hat, and shiny badge are all aspects of presence. If the presence is sufficient, you rarely have to use physical force. That's a good thing.

Few rookie officers are taught much beyond this. What skill they develop in projecting presence is learned on the job or by watching older officers.

There is also a danger here—many rookies and even some experienced officers come to count on the power of the badge and the uniform. Most people quit being bad when they see an officer. Most follow directions. Some officers come to expect this and are surprised—and injured—when they presume threats will comply.

A small number of officers expect the uniform to do the job for them. We call it 'hiding behind the badge.' It doesn't work very well. As an officer, you need to develop the skills, experience, and reputation to earn respect. That is real presence.

Level 2: Verbal

There is more skill and more variation at the verballevel than at all other levels combined. SWAT tactics don't approach the complexity of a good debate, much less the nuance of talking down an emotionally disturbed person (EDP) in crisis, or eliciting a good description from a traumatized child.

In a law enforcement career, you will never run into a useless piece of information. You might discuss the philosophies of Locke and Rousseau with protesters; global economics with a pimp; mathematics with an arsonist; and string theory with a murderer—all in the same month. Building rapport is a matter of common ground and a skill.

Prior to a Use of Force, if there is time, we try to talk the threat into complying. Ask, Advise, Order, and Check is a common and useful system.

Ask: "Sir, you are under arrest and you must go to jail. Please turn around and let me handcuff you." Asking does no harm. It works a surprisingly large percentage of time. At this stage, if you are polite, it is hard for the threat to convince himself that you are the enemy and he is righteous. 'Please' *is* a magic word, just as they said in kindergarten.

Advise: "Sir, if you do not let me handcuff you, I will use force against you." In the advise step, you let the threat know the consequences of not complying: sometimes it is force, sometimes that they may be considered a suspect, or just that someone he or she cares about may be disappointed. This book is about force, but force isn't always *or even usually* the best option.

Sometimes it helps to display or describe the kind of force you are contemplating. One of my colleagues, Steve Pina, actually gives a short class on Taser to the threat, with good success. Without displaying the force option, I have very rarely had the threat comply at this step. Be aware that threatening to use a level of force that you could not justify is, in itself, excessive force. At this stage, you are still being polite and it is harder for the threat to make it personal.

Order: "Sir! I am giving you a direct order! Turn around and put your hands behind your back now!" I don't know why this works so much more often than the 'advise' stage, but it does. Maybe it is the shift from polite to command voice.

Check: "Sir, you are telling me I have to use force. Thank you for being clear. It makes the paperwork much easier." Then, if practical, you walk away. Frequently, within a few seconds the threat realizes that he has not only given permission but also demanded whatever comes next. If you can afford to give them a little time, most threats rethink things at this stage and decide to comply.

Any verbal commands given to the threat should be simple. Some of the criminals that an officer deals with will not be honor students, and might even be impaired by recreational chemicals. No big words.

No complicated sentences. When possible, use positive (do) speech, e.g., "put your hands out" and not negative, e.g., "don't hide your hands." Tell the threat what to do as opposed to telling the threat what not to do.

The orders should always be given by ONE officer. I feel sorry for the poor criminal facing two guns when one of the officers is yelling, "Don't move!" and the other is yelling, "Get on the floor! Get down!" Even if the orders are not contradictory, multiple voices are confusing.

Ideally, verbal commands should be professional: no anger, no

Experts. Whenever there is a media-rich Use of Force, experts will come out of the woodwork to tell anyone who will listen that if the officers only had a "little more training" in dealing with emotionally disturbed people or the mentally ill, or the particular (after the fact) diagnosis of the particular threat, the force could have been avoided.

This will come up more in section three, but let's get this straight here: These experts are largely speaking from the safety of their desks. Counseling tens of thousands of patients in a clinical setting *starts* with someone who was stable enough to get to the clinical setting. Calming people who are emotionally distraught and might cry or threaten is not the same as talking someone down from a frothing, enraged, psychotic break.*

Patients listen. Universally, they want something the clinical expert can give: comfort, solace, or (in the criminal world) a slip of paper or report that will absolve the patient from bad acts or another slip of paper for drugs. The experts are experts in dealing with people who are at least stable enough to listen. Take away that condition and much of their expertise becomes irrelevant.

Training is good. Insight is good. As the officer develops more experience, he can do more with knowledge. But whatever is learned and no matter from whom, training will always be a tool, not an answer.

* Sometimes a person becomes so angry, fearful, or stressed that they do things that make no sense, things that no one would normally consider—like taking hostages in an attempt to get custody of a child. It's a cop term, not a diagnosis.

threats, and no profanity. You can make a case that profanity is closer to the "native language" of the average threat. You can show that sometimes, especially if you have not used profanity so far, a single example can get the threat to take you seriously.

There is more going on, though. Force situations do not happen in a vacuum. Every action the officer makes is not only accomplishing the goal but is also creating witnesses. A witness who sees an officer grab a suspect by the throat and slam him against the wall will interpret the act very differently if he hears the officer say, "Don't do it you son of a bitch! I'm warning you! I'll beat the shit out of you!" than if he hears the same officer say, "Sir, don't swallow those drugs! You could die!" Same actions, same reasons, entirely different witness perceptions.

The application of force is one of the officer's professional duties and he must do it like a professional . . . no anger . . . no sarcasm. Use calm professionalism because this is a job. Keep the ego out of it.

Force Continuum

<table>
<tr><th>Level of Force</th><th colspan="3">Method of Force</th><th>Level of Resistance</th><th>Threat</th></tr>
<tr><td>VI Deadly</td><td colspan="3">Any force readily capable of causing death or serious physical injury</td><td>Lethal</td><td rowspan="3">Resistive</td></tr>
<tr><td>V Serious physical control</td><td>Impact weapon
Focused blow
Electronic stun devices*
Mace (CN/CS)
*Nova, Stun Shield, etc.</td><td rowspan="2">PEPPER SPRAY</td><td rowspan="2">TASER</td><td rowspan="2">Ominous
Active
Static</td></tr>
<tr><td>IV Physical control</td><td>Hair takedown
Joint takedown
Digital control
Joint come-along
Pressure points
Temporary restraints</td></tr>
<tr><td>III Physical contact</td><td colspan="3">Escort position
Directional contact</td><td rowspan="2">Verbal</td><td rowspan="2">Undecided</td></tr>
<tr><td>II Verbal communication</td><td colspan="3">Direct order
Questioning
Persuasion</td></tr>
<tr><td>I Presence</td><td colspan="3">Display of force option
Body language/demeanor
Identification of authority</td><td>None</td><td>Complying</td></tr>
</table>

A force continuum used in training by Multnomah County, Oregon 2007. Note levels of force, force options and levels of resistance.

National Use of Force Framework
Le cadre national de l'emploi de la force

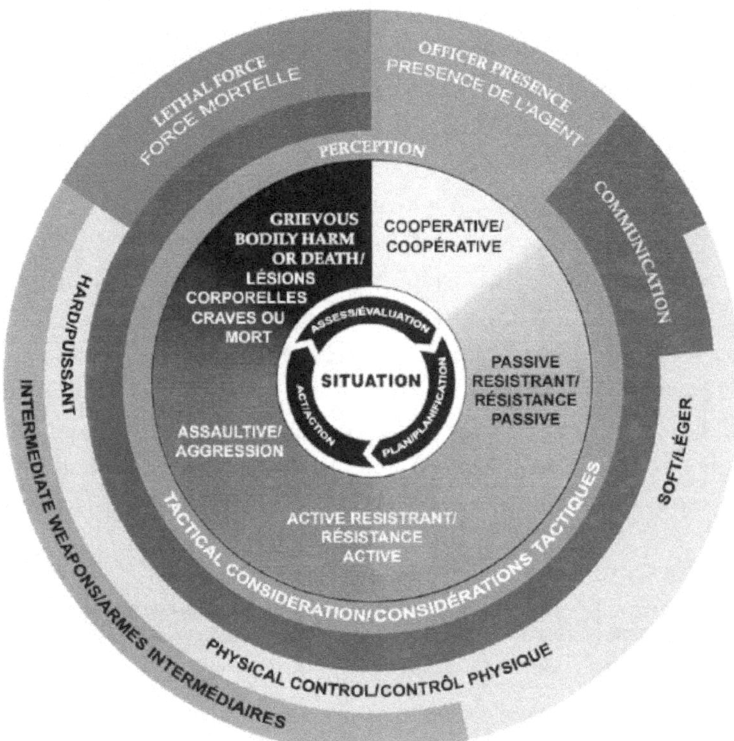

The officer continuously assesses the situation and acts in a reasonable manner to ensure officer and public safety.

L'agent doit continuellement évaluer la situation et agir de manière raisonnable afin d'assurer sa propre sécurité et celle du public.

Example of a Force Decision Framework laid out as available options rather than levels.

There is much more to learn, but the rookie will learn it on the job through trial and error.

Level 3: Touch

Touch on the surface is simple. The hand on the shoulder to establish rapport, the hand on the elbow to steer a drunk in the right direction. It can be reassuring. It can be as comforting as a hug shared with someone who has just been rescued. It can de-escalate situations that are beyond words.

It can also go very, very bad. Will that hand on the shoulder comfort the grieving survivor? Or trigger memories of abuse that the officer has no way of knowing? The danger lies in the fact that the officer is very close—well within reach should the threat decide to attack. If that should happen, the officer has already misjudged the threat's intent.

Level 4: Pain Compliance and Physical Control

Level 4 includes all of the techniques that have a good chance of getting the threat to go along with a relatively low risk of injury—things such as joint locks, pressure points, take downs, and, in some jurisdictions, OC (Oleoresin Capsicum aka pepper spray), and Taser.

The goal at Level 4 is primarily compliance, getting the threat to go along with the program because to do otherwise hurts, but the officer also attempts to establish control at Level 4 to prevent the threat escalating to a higher level of resistance. Taking a threat to the ground, for instance, removes half of his potential mobility and makes it very difficult for him to strike. Thus, there is a mix of techniques here—pure pain techniques such as pressure points and also techniques that give the officer mechanical advantage to prevent or force movement from the threat.

Applying Level 4 early often preempts an officer's need to use a higher level of force. An officer who has reason to believe (can articulate Intent, Means, and Opportunity) that he is about to be attacked does not need to wait for the attack to manifest. If, as soon as I sense a situation is about to go bad, I sweep the threat's legs out, spin him to his belly, and kneel on his elbow and neck, I will be able to handcuff him with little risk of injury. If, however, I wait until he swings, we have a fistfight with all the possibilities of concussion and broken teeth and broken knuckles and bleeding.

Pure pain techniques are used for one of three reasons: bargaining, to draw a specific movement, or to distract the threat.

Bargaining is obvious, but rarely overtly stated: "If you quit struggling and let me put handcuffs on, I will quit bending your fingers or pressing on this pressure point."

Certain pressure points have relatively reliable flinch responses. There is one on the jaw that I use to turn a threat face down. There is a combination of two that I like, one in the elbow, the other beneath the jaw that sets up a sweep.

Lastly, a sharp, unexpected pain can make the threat freeze for a second and might buy you time to do something else.

The problem with pain is that it is personal, idiosyncratic, and unreliable. Not everyone responds to pain the same way. People in a psychotic break, under the influence of drugs or alcohol, emotionally disturbed, or just really angry or afraid do not feel pain the same way as a healthy, calm, sane person.

If pain doesn't work, and you can't achieve control with these techniques (and very few of the techniques give absolute control separate from pain), and the threat continues to resist, it is almost guaranteed that you will have to resort to a higher level of force to end the situation.

Too many of the people officers are required to use force on fall into one of those pain-dulled categories: drunk or drugged; an altered state of consciousness; or just really, really angry or afraid: The very people the lowest level of force is least likely to work on.

Level-4 Tools: Taser and OC. In a lot of ways, the Holy Grail of Law Enforcement has been a quest for a tool that could be used at a distance (safe for the officer) that was as likely as a handgun to put the threat down and did no more injury than the level four techniques. The closest that modern technology has brought us has been OC and the Taser.

OC is a food product, a highly refined hot pepper sauce that can be sprayed or squirted into the face of a threat. It feels about the way you would expect rubbing pureed habaneras peppers in your eyes would feel. Your nose runs, your eyes squeeze shut. You can breathe just fine, but some people come to believe that they are suffocating and panic. Most people feel no further need to fight and will do almost anything for the opportunity to wash the stuff out of their eyes.

Is it effective? Usually. Most people respond to pain normally and OC hurts, so it works as a pain-compliance tool most of the time. Some few panic and they fight harder, which increases the risk of death from cardiac or respiratory arrest. In almost all cases, the threat will be unable to open his eyes, and it is almost always easier to subdue a threat who cannot see.

In a very small number of cases, usually on the Excited Delirium side (see section 3.6, "The Nightmare Threat"), OC has no effect at all. I had to deal with one threat who was sprayed with five large canisters of OC (called 'magnums' or 'party canisters') with no effect whatsoever. He didn't even shut his eyes . . . just hung on to his two shanks and screamed for someone to come close enough for him to kill. Another threat just continued to drive his own head into the wall, not noticing the OC at all. A third stared at me, scooped a handful of pepper foam from his cheek, and started to eat it. I have heard of one threat who scooped up the foam and threw it at the officers, blinding them.

There was one unintended effect of OC in all of those cases. It made the threat slippery. OC is an oil.

The Taser is the latest "evil machine" that the media and activists love to hate. It is scary and new and electric, and its advent happened to coincide with the exploding popularity of YouTube and other Internet video sites.

The Taser hurts unbelievably. I have a relatively high tolerance for pain. When I scale pain, my top two used to be either recovering from frostbite in my hands (so bad I whimpered for almost an hour, unable to stop the noises coming out of my throat) or running on a broken fibula. Or maybe getting my fingernail melted through so the doctor could relieve pressure on a crushing injury.

The Taser blew all of those away. It lasts for five seconds. For about the first three my mind was completely blank—nothing in the brain but pain. Then, I started to be able to think and decided to count slowly until it was over. I thought, "This whole experience lasts five seconds and I must be halfway through, right?" Counting as slowly as I could, I got to twelve in those 2 to 3 seconds.

Then it was over. I was fine. There were two barbed needles in my back, a quarter-inch deep that needed to be pulled out, and that was it. As soon as the cycle was over, I was good to go, fully capable of either complying or fighting again.

Obviously, I like the Taser. The guy in the OC example who was driving his head into a brick wall? I saved his life by tasing him. It causes more pain than a joint lock or pressure point with far less risk of injury. It applies a level of pain that is legendary in the criminal community. It does so at a distance that is safe for the officer. Most of the time, it causes the muscles to seize-up and the threat drops—which can't be said for a handgun.

A Taser is not the same as the stun gun, sometimes erroneously called a Taser, on TV. It fires two darts attached by wires to a battery in the Taser. The top wire shoots out straight and the bottom dart is angled slightly downward. The maximum range of the wires was 21 feet, but a new model cartridge increases that to 35 feet.

When the darts impact, an electric charge shoots down the wires and between the two probes. The electrical charge is 50,000 volts, but only 2.1 milliamps. The charge lasts for five seconds. If the threat is still a threat, you can squeeze the trigger for additional five-second cycles, as long as the probes (darts) stay attached.

Is the Taser the grail? Not yet. There are still problems. Most are single shot devices, though Taser International recently released a 3-shot version. If you miss, it turns into a relatively fragile hand-to-hand weapon. You can still deliver a shock with it, but because the contact points are not spread as wide as the darts would be, it is less effective, causing both less pain and less muscle "freeze."

It has a limited range. Because of the angle of the second dart, it will not be effective if the threat is behind cover. If the threat isn't standing upright, the officer has to remember to angle the weapon to match the threat's angle or the second dart will miss.

The Taser is not perfectly safe—no force option is. However, in my experience it is much safer than even very low levels of physical force. Some people have died after a Taser was deployed. The deaths are likely not caused by the Taser.

In 2006, Amnesty International (AI) published a study implicating the Taser in 152 deaths in the United States. Here's a piece of

Any use of force can appear shocking to the uninitiated. Many citizens in the U.S. have never seen the physical injuries that can result when force is used. But almost all have felt pain.

I've been involved in several discussions on Taser use, especially incidents that have been widely reported on the Internet. In many cases, especially when the Taser was used on someone who was physically fragile, people were very concerned, wondering why the officer couldn't have resolved the situation with physical force.

The officer could have. But physical force, even at low levels, involves take downs, joint locks, shoving and forcing people to move. In the use of the taser, the concerned citizens were seeing a tool that causes great pain. 'Tool' and 'great' both trigger a presumption that the force applied is greater than more primitive weapons.

Often, officers don't see it the same way. We have seen (and many of us have suffered from) injuries cause by low levels of force. Officers do not equate pain and injury. Often, the choice of Taser or OC is based on an assessment that despite the pain, these are the methods with the least likelihood of *causing injury*. A runny nose and watery eyes from OC, or two needle sticks one-quarter inch deep from the Taser, versus the possibility of fragile bones breaking, scrapes, bruises, or concussions.

advice—when you see a study or a brief like this, don't just read the headline. If you care, get a copy of the study and read the whole thing for yourself.

According to Amnesty International's report, only 23 of the coroners listed the Taser as even a *possible contributory* cause of death. One of the cases states that the Taser may have contributed to the fatal abnormal heartbeat *in addition to the other causes of meth and bleeding out from a cut wrist*. Only seven listed the cause of death as Taser.

Just seven deaths in five years. The agenda is clear in a single interesting phrase from the report where AI states ". . . tasers in dart-firing mode may be a preferable alternative to deadly force . . ." Wow. *May* be? So guns are generally preferred? Death and injury is better than pain? The mind boggles . . .

But I repeat—read the study for yourself.

Level 5: Damage

Level 5 is authorized when the officer is in danger, when Level 5 has failed to work, or when level four is unlikely to work.* Level 5 is the "focused blows"—punching, kicking, striking with batons, and also breaking joints. These actions are designed to do damage, ideally the minimum amount of damage that will convince the threat to quit fighting OR that will render the threat unable to fight.

Just as pain is idiosyncratic, to some extent so is damage. Escalating force from Level 4 to Level 5 is increasing the stakes, hoping the person will choose to quit fighting. Some people show amazing will and can fight long after others would have given up.

A person can keep fighting even with extreme damage, and people have done so after being shot in the head or in the heart. In order to actually do enough damage that a person could not fight, their brain must be shut down, their spine severed, or every long bone in the body would have to be broken. Even then, most could still pull a trigger.

> In 2003, Sgt. Marcus Young, of the Ukiah, California, Police Department was attacked by a man who tried to stab him. Sgt. Young grabbed the knife arm, got off line . . . and was shot by the .38 caliber revolver the threat, Neal Beckman, had in his other hand.
>
> Beckman emptied the revolver, striking Sgt. Young in the face with the first round and in the chest, back, and arm with others. Young's weapon arm was mangled and he could not draw his own weapon.
>
> A security officer, unarmed Brett Schott, attempted to help, and Beckman stabbed him high in the left chest. Schott's lung tissue was visible through the wound.

* This is often a judgment call, but generally, if a small officer is faced with 250 pounds of muscle, he or she can usually make an educated guess that wrestling will not work.

> Different jurisdictions have very different policies. In some, a level of force is a level of force and the mechanism with which it is delivered is irrelevant. In other words, if focused blows are authorized, policy does not distinguish between a fist, a boot, a baton, or a "found weapon" such as a telephone handset, a radio, a stick, or a rock.
>
> Other jurisdictions severely limit the officer's options by prohibiting the use of any tool or technique that is not specifically authorized. An officer who hit a suspect with his radio, for instance, would have acted outside of policy, even if he would have been authorized to use a baton (or even a handgun).

Most men, shot in the face, chest, and back would have curled up and died. Unable to draw a weapon, many would have given up. Young didn't. When Beckman started to get into the patrol car—not to get away, but to access the assault rifle racked there—Young saw his chance and ordered his seventeen-year-old, unarmed cadet, Julian Covella, to unholster Young's weapon, and place it in Young's left hand.

Young's left arm was damaged, but he could still pull a trigger. He engaged and killed Beckman.

Sgt. Young is extraordinarily dedicated and it is rare to find a threat with the same dedication, but they do exist. Just keep in mind that most focused blows, as they are taught, are intended to do minimal damage. For instance, officers are taught that the preferred targets to strike with a baton are the big muscle groups of the legs and arms. Striking the joints or exposed bones are a distant second choice and striking the head, neck, and lower torso are last resort tactics. This ordering of priorities is the exact opposite of the order of effectiveness. As taught, most focused blows are a psychological extension of pain compliance, raising the stakes to damage in an attempt to get the threat to quit.

Level 6: Deadly Force

Deadly force can be defined as any force used in a manner in which it is intended to cause death or great bodily injury.* That is another of those very long, very legal sentences. A take down is Level 4; however, knocking someone down in front of an oncoming car (deliberately) is deadly force, Level 6.

If the officer were to take someone to the ground and the person hit a rib, which broke and punctured the liver or lung, 'great bodily harm' resulted . . . but because there was no intention to cause the injury, the action is Level 4.

There is no level of force that is perfectly safe. It is impossible to know the health condition of the threat or to control all of the variables in the fight. Joint locks and come-along holds are generally very safe, but some threats will not feel the pain or will fight against the pain and dislocate their own joints. Some threats may have cardiac or vascular conditions that make it possible for heart attacks or aneurisms to occur if their heart rate increases. Any time a threat is taken to the ground, a generally safe strategy and one that increases control, he may land on something sharp or hard, unseen by the officer. There is a rare medical condition in which ribs spontaneously break and can puncture the lungs resulting in a spontaneous pneumothorax. Someone with this condition is usually unaware of it and can die just from jogging. Can the officer be expected to predict this condition?

Great bodily harm includes actions that put life in danger, that cripple or could potentially cripple, or that could blind the threat. This is variable, and something that in each case lawyers could argue over endlessly. Is a lifetime back injury or a bum knee 'great bodily harm'?

1.7 Factors and Circumstances

The level of resistance (none, verbal, static, active, ominous, lethal) generally dictates the level of force (presence, verbal, touch, pain compliance/physical control, damage, lethal) that is authorized

* Some agencies use the phrase ". . . likely to cause," a change of a single word that can make the officers responsible for actions they did not intend.

for the officer to use. There are a number of things that modify what otherwise might seem like a simple decision.

HARD TRUTH #6

> *There will never be a simple formula to give clear answers to how much force is enough. Force incidents are chaos and you can't write a cookie-cutter answer to chaos.*

These modifiers are generally divided into differences between the officer and the threat (referred to as Officer-Threat Factors) and the Influential Circumstances surrounding the fight.

Officer-Threat Factors: There are variables between people that affect how much force is likely to be needed. Some of the factors include size and strength, numbers, skill, age, gender, and mental state.

Size and strength: It is harder to cuff a big, strong resisting threat than to cuff a small, weak resisting threat. It is easier for a big, strong officer to take down a given threat than for a smaller, weaker officer to take down the same threat. If an officer coming to a call can see that he is clearly outmatched, he can and should access the force option that will put the odds solidly in his favor.

Numbers: If the officer is outnumbered by multiple ominous threats and the situation goes hands-on, he is almost automatically in a deadly force situation. Restraint techniques on one threat leave you completely exposed to any other threats. Damage techniques sometimes do not have a quick enough effect to remove one threat completely from the fight and few officers can engage one threat while defending themselves from a second. Fighting two or more people successfully rarely works outside of Hollywood.

Factors work both ways. If multiple officers are present, they should be able to use less force to affect the arrest than a single officer would alone. If that seems counterintuitive—that multiple officers mean less force and less risk of injury to the threat—think it through. You are an officer, alone in an abandoned building, looking at a 240-pound man wanted on warrants for violent felonies. If he fights and you are alone, you are required to use the least amount of force that you believe will get him in cuffs—preferably without injury. If you don't have a Taser, that almost certainly means a baton, and that almost certainly means he will be struck and that almost certainly means injuries. Maybe only bruises, but possibly broken bones or a concussion.

Four officers facing the same threat can each grab a limb, bear him down with weight or a sweep, and force his arms into position for handcuffing. What would be almost certainly a high-level and dangerous use of force for one officer can be handled at a lower level by multiple officers.

Is this perfectly safe? No, not for anybody. It is just *safer*, but for reasons mentioned earlier, no use of force is completely safe for the officer or the threat.

Skill: If you know, or find out very quickly, that a threat is a better fighter than you are, don't fight him. If a locally famous street brawler has cleared out an entire bar, you don't go in there trying to prove who is tougher. Change the game. This is when you use tools (Taser, OC, less lethal munitions, baton) or numbers (never be afraid to call for back-up) or take time to devise a plan and try to get surprise. If a threat has no idea how to fight, you can sometimes just spin him, push him into a wall, and put cuffs on while he is confused. Try that on a skilled fighter and you will be badly hurt.

The reversal—an officer with decades in martial arts might well be expected to use a hands-on technique in a situation where another officer would need a tool.

Age: In the academy, recruits will be hammered with anti-discrimination classes and messages. They will be told it is evil to

> Anything presented in class, anything written here, is a generalization. *Generally*, an eighty-year-old will not fight as hard and will give up easier than a twenty-year old. Generally. But I know some very tough, very mean old people and some very weak, very cowardly young men. How influential each of the factors will be varies in each case. This is one of the big contributors to Hard Truth #6.

discriminate based on age or gender. Then, in Use of Force, they will be ordered to discriminate.

That's fine, because this is common sense. With a few exceptions, a ninety-year-old doesn't fight as hard or suck up damage like a twenty-something. When we hear of a nursing home resident being tased, the presumption is that it probably wasn't necessary. Presumptions are rarely completely correct, but still . . . the officer probably doesn't need the same level of force to handcuff a resisting geriatric or grade-schooler as it would take for an adult in the prime of life.

Officers change as they age, too. I don't heal like I used to. Some of my joints catch and click and hurt. I really would prefer not to have any more concussions. Consequently, in my forties I don't fight like I did in my twenties, and I am not expected to. Which is a good thing.

Gender is one of the few "one-way" factors. Male and female threats fight very differently and both are dangerous. Generally, men are stronger and have more power when they try to hurt you. It stands to reason that bigger, stronger people can do more damage. On the other hand, women have fewer socially conditioned predispositions on how they are "supposed" to fight. Women just try to injure you. Scratching at eyes and biting and using weapons are more likely (in my experience) with women than with men. Male and female threats are dangerous in different ways, but both are dangerous and the gender of the threat makes little difference in force justification.

The gender of the officer can make quite a bit of difference, however. Unlike threats, male and female officers are expected to fight pretty much the same way, using what they were taught by their agencies, or at the academy. Because they are theoretically limited to the same techniques, the fact that female officers tend to be smaller and have less strength than men often justifies a female officer using a level of force that a male officer would have more difficulty justifying.

Mental State: One of the most important factors in any fight is *will.* More important than size, or strength, or tactical advantage, is the will to fight: to endure, to keep going, and to win. Fighting is far more mental than physical, and most fights or force incidents are ended not when the threat is beaten, but when the threat chooses to quit fighting. When he or she loses *will.*

> I will reference altered mental states a lot in this book. Sorry if it sounds repetitive. It is important because, to some extent, people are self-referencing. We judge from our own experience what others are likely to do, think, or feel.
>
> It is important for rookie officers, or anyone who deals with violence, to understand that our normal expectations are tied to a baseline that is NOT normal in many force situations.

This is easier to see with normal people, but normal people rarely fight with cops. Often when an officer uses force, the threat is in an altered mental state: On drugs, drunk, having a psychotic break, or just extremely angry or scared. These states can change the threat's willingness to take or deal damage, deaden his sensitivity to pain, alter his or her normal idea of right and wrong, and greatly change the point at which the threat would normally choose to quit fighting.

If a threat can't feel pain or won't respond to it, the pain compliance aspect of Level 4 is off the table. A joint lock will not get a surrender. The joint may break as the officer, who was conditioned in training to gradually increase force until the threat complies, increases force without getting compliance.

If the officer needs to gain control and the threat does not feel pain, it almost guarantees an injury or a fight, often with many officers, to exhaustion.

Influential Circumstances. There are various aspects of where and when a fight happens, or how it develops, that can change what would be an acceptable level of force. These include the presence of a weapon; injury, exhaustion and disability; environmental hazards; inability to disengage; surprise; ground level; previous experience; and special knowledge.

If a weapon is involved, the danger is much higher than if the threat is unarmed. That's obvious and is subsumed in the "Means" aspect of Intent, Means, and Opportunity. If the subject has the means to shoot or stab you the response is different from if he only has the means to insult you. Weapons can alter the equation, even when they

> There is always a weapon in reach when an officer uses physical force on a threat. The weapons on the officer's belt can be taken away and used against him or her. An actively resisting threat can become a lethal threat in an instant.

are not in the threat's possession. A threat standing within reach of a collection of kitchen knives is a more dangerous threat than one in an empty room. The officer can justify using higher levels of force to prevent access to the available weapons.

Normally an officer restrains a threat's movement to bring the threat into custody or to stop the threat from doing something, such as flushing evidence. This is active resistance (movement) and generally authorizes Physical Control.

If the movement is toward a weapon, however, the motivation is to prevent the situation from escalating to a potentially deadly encounter.

Injury, exhaustion, and disability decrease an officer's ability to effectively apply force. If an officer is in a long fight and the threat shows no sign of tiring and the officer is so exhausted he can't continue, the officer must use a higher level of force. If an officer is injured, he will not be able to do what he has been doing effectively. Lastly, an officer with a disability, such as a bad back, will not be able to fight as effectively as a fully fit officer.

HARD TRUTH #7

If you become injured or exhausted while at a certain level of force, it is a sure sign you are using too low a level. You are losing! If you keep using something that is already not working, you will fail utterly. This is not a game.

Like almost all of the factors, this works both ways. As the threat becomes exhausted or injured, it requires less force to achieve or maintain control.

Environmental hazards indicate things that endanger the officer separate from the fight itself. Most fights are chaotic and luck can play a major role. If the officer is in environmental danger—fighting in water or on the edge of a roof or in traffic for instance—he needs to finish the encounter quickly, for both his safety and the threat's. Higher levels of force end things more quickly than lower levels of force. If the danger is extreme, the need to get out of the environment may justify deadly force.

Inability to disengage: An officer is rarely *required* to make an arrest. In general, if he or she is likely to lose, to be beaten or killed, it is not only possible but often prudent to get to safety and call for assistance. This is not playtime. The stakes are high.

If this option is removed, if the officer is trapped, the fact that any force in which he might lose could easily result in his death can justify more force.

Conversely, a barricaded threat is also trapped, which justifies handling a potentially deadly force situation with crisis negotiators, a Level 2 (verbal) intervention. Think about that—a threat with weapons, barricaded in a house and threatening to shoot anyone he sees is clearly a lethal threat. He has the Intent (threatening to kill anyone he can see), the Means (a firearm), and the Opportunity (a hunting rifle can send a bullet more than a thousand meters with enough power to kill) to pose a lethal threat to many people. Using a sniper to neutralize the threat is easy to justify . . . but the first option is to talk and it works often.

Surprise. A judicious and proper application of force is based on a thorough and unbiased analysis of the situation leading to a careful decision about the best course of action. Time for this simply does not exist in an ambush. Figuring out the situation and choosing a response takes time. In an ambush, time is damage. By the time the officer makes a decision, he might be physically incapable of carrying the decision out.

If you are taking damage, you need to use as much force as you can to get safe enough to assess. Survival first and assessment second. Survival is the first Golden Rule.

Conversely, officers use surprise as much as possible. The primary reason that joint locks and takedowns work is that we don't give the threat time to get ready. He just has to say he wants to hurt us; we don't have to wait for him to warm up and start boxing.

Entry teams (the guys who break down the doors in drug houses and warrant arrests) are often going into fortified places with heavily armed people who hate cops. If they go in with enough surprise, speed, and noise, the bad guys are often knocked down and disarmed while their mouths are still hanging open.

Ground Level: Officers take threats to the ground to increase control. The earth cuts off 180 degrees of the threat's possible movement, his weasel room. If a threat takes an officer to the ground, it is also to increase control. Controlling an officer—with all of the available weapons that can be stripped off the uniform belt and the ability to do killing damage with kicks or bricks—is a bad thing. This relates to Injury/Exhaustion: If a threat has taken you to the ground, you are losing. You need to do whatever you need to do, whatever you can, to survive—either to create space and escape or to disable the threat.

Previous experience comes up more often in local policing and corrections than you realize. We know most of our fighters. We also know which ones will put on a good show, then get submissive as soon as their bluff is called.* If you are aware that a threat always fights, it is prudent to show up with a Taser at the ready. If the officer knows the threat is usually armed, the officer should have his own weapon (preferably a rifle or shotgun, and back-up) at the ready.

Special knowledge is similar. If the officer notices something or the threat divulges something that changes the situation, the officer is allowed to take that information into consideration. Even if it is not true. (criminals often, even usually, lie). If someone claims to be a black belt, a Navy SEAL, or has a USMC tattoo, the officer will likely use a different level of force than if the threat says he's undergoing treatment for bone cancer.

1.8 The Threat Is in Control

This is another concept that is hard for civilians to understand: The threat is in control of every aspect of a Use of Force.

* Not always. There have been some severe officer injuries caused by threats who the officer had categorized as "all talk" or "not a fighter" and the officer let his guard down.

It seems counter-intuitive. On one side, you have the police with belts full of weapons, radios, back-up, and, theoretically, the weight and influence of all of civilization behind them. On the other side, you have the threat. Sometimes armed, often not. Sometimes impaired with drugs, alcohol, or mental illness. We see the disparity in power, and even the disparity in judgment, and assume the responsibility lies with the person in power. The smart one.

Fighting bad guys isn't like rolling with your buddies in martial arts classes. Sometimes it's dangerous. It's usually messy and almost always stinks. The cops know that. Not one person I work with gets up in the morning and says, "Hey, with any luck, I'll get in a big fight with a crazy tweaker and his four friends! And they'll have oozing sores all over, and ooooh, maybe it can happen in a shooting gallery with used hypodermic needles all over the place and puddles of urine! Whooo hoo!"

Or "Damn, it's really hard to get vacation time in the summer. Hey, if I shoot someone, I get some days off for psych! Of course, I'll probably need the psych, and my career and all my personal possessions will be on the line from the eventual lawsuit. There might be nightmares and stuff and I'll probably get divorced but I really want to go fishing this weekend."

So, the first element of a Use of Force: The threat makes it happen. I want to be left alone to eat donuts and talk to my friends all day. I wouldn't even be responding unless someone called me and said that there was a bad guy up to something, or I see the threat being bad.

The next element is even easier—for the most part, unless it's really outrageous, all the threat has to do is STOP BEING BAD WHEN HE SEES A COP. Really, how hard is that? In the jail, if I see someone breaking a rule, I catch the person's eye, maybe shake my head, and he stops. If he doesn't stop, I'll have to do something. Usually, talking is enough.

Even if the behavior is outrageous—hostages, assault, murder—the threat stops being bad (drops the weapon, puts his hands up, and complies with orders) and there's still no use of force. I'm not saying that there aren't bad guys who I've wanted to hurt, there have been. But the arrest, the paperwork, the likelihood of conviction all go easier without the force. Most officers are professional and won't give in to the anger.

Time is a critical limiting factor. If the threat is in the process of shooting someone, there is no time for making eye contact or talking. The officer must tackle or shoot, depending on which is faster. Presentation is another factor—someone screaming or ignoring you or being (or pretending to be) in a psychotic break can also remove the verbal skills from the table.

Simple as that: The threat chooses whether or not he will respond to the officer's presence or the officer's attempt to communicate. He also chooses if communication won't work. The officer has a duty to act and if communication won't work (or fails), the officer must use force. The force starts because the threat makes it start.

How much force is used? The minimum level the officer reasonably believes will safely end the situation. It's a guess and the threat supplies the clues. If he claims to be a multiple black belt or a SEAL, he gets hit harder. If he claims to be a peaceful protester but needs to be moved, finger locks or pepper spray (pain compliance tools that rarely cause injury) are the preferred response.

Most importantly, the threat decides if the level of force the officer is using is enough. If I put a finger lock on a threat, and it doesn't work, I'll have to use something else. Something more. It escalates, but the threat dictates the escalation.

The last piece: When is the Use of Force (UofF) over? When the threats decide it is. Here's a secret that applies to people and life and armies: people are almost never beaten—they give up. Until blood loss is so extreme that the brain begins to shut down as in the hemorrhagic shock of a shooting or the threat is physically shattered, the decision to fight or to quit fighting is a choice.

So the threat decides when he gives up. What level of force or pain does he have to endure before he can allow himself to be handcuffed and still maintain his 'manly dignity'? That sounded flip, but some of the worst uses of force are from upstanding citizens who think that they aren't *real* criminals (only drinking and driving, or beating the wife that they "own"), and they fight as a matter of honor.

So, to sum up—if the threat decides *when* force is going to be used, and *how much* force is going to be used, *and* when it will stop . . . who is in charge?

1.9 Scaling Force

Fights are dynamic and chaotic situations. A simple escort hold, walking a drunk off the premises can turn into a knife fight or a struggle for your weapon in an instant. Or you and several other officers could be fighting against a large, vicious threat who is acting completely inhuman and have him suddenly go limp.

Changing conditions require changes in the force that you apply. So might changing assessment of the conditions: If the situation is going well, you might be able to use less force; if you are losing, you need more.

There are factors that affect these situations and basic principles to keep in mind.

First and foremost, force is used to accomplish a goal, to gain control. It is used either to make a threat do something or to stop a threat from doing something. It is not used for payback or to prove dominance. Force is never used to inflict punishment.

There are two reasons for this, one based on theory and the classroom, the other based on experience.

First, the officer learns the law and policy on force. Force within that policy is legal and appropriate. Cross those lines and you are committing assault, possibly manslaughter or even murder. As an officer you are paid, trained, and sworn to be one of the good guys. Always. No matter how bad a day you have had or how putrid a piece of human predator you are dealing with, cross that line, use the wrong force or use force for the wrong reason, and you are the criminal.

Second, and this is not theory, but some officers never realize this: Criminals have a specific worldview. *Those with power, take. If you can get over, you get over. The world is divided into weak and strong, victims and predators*. Career criminals believe the world works this way and that everyone knows it—the "good" citizens are only too stupid or too afraid to act on it. Whenever an officer crosses that line, it merely confirms the criminal's beliefs and they take it as proof that society itself and the protectors of society are pure hypocrisy.

> Generally, there are two ways that an officer gets in trouble in a force situation.
>
> Excessive force is using force from a higher level on the force continuum than can be justified.
>
> The second, unnecessary force, is more common in my experience. When the officer uses force in a situation where a reasonable officer would not, the force may be found unnecessary. If the officer actually provides Means or Opportunity (e.g., "You want to fight me? Okay, I'll take your cuffs off."), then unnecessary force is very clear.

"Punishment" is the strange idea that you can make a bad person into a better person through pain. You can't. You only accomplish two things. You convince them that they were right, all along, and you guarantee that they will hurt someone else. After whatever beating you administer, they will feel a need to get their manhood back and will choose a victim, often their wife or child, to hurt. Experienced officers know this. Rookies need to know it, too.

This is the official word: Deliberate misuse of force will be investigated and disciplined internally, criminally, or both.

Before escalating force, sometimes before even engaging in it, the officer must ask himself if it is worth the risk of injury (to self, threat, and bystanders) to even engage.

In 1985, the U.S. Supreme Court ruled on the case of Tennessee v. Garner.* A skinny, 16-year-old burglar had run away from officers and they shot him in the back. The U.S. Supreme Court said that was wrong. Well, duh.

It's hard to explain how profound an effect this decision had on our culture and the law enforcement community. In less than three decades as of this writing, but even in six years' time, when I started my career in 1991, the impact of the decision was simply obvious—you don't shoot people who don't present an immediate threat.

The thing was, the Garner decision was a landmark. Up until

* Tennessee v. Garner, 471 U.S. 1 (1985).

then, and going back to English Common Law (before our Constitution, before the Magna Carta), running from an agent of the law was reason in and of itself to justify deadly force. If someone were to be taken into custody, he or she would go into custody even if it meant using lethal force to enforce a littering statute.

In the movie *It's a Wonderful Life*, Jimmy Stewart, drunk, wrecks his car. When an officer confronts him, Stewart runs away and the officer fires on him. When the movie was made, that was simply the way things were. There is nothing in the movie about the morality of that issue; it wasn't questioned. It seems surreal from our modern point of view.

So even beyond whether the threat's demeanor and actions justify a certain level of force, the officer has to look at the big picture and decide if the goal—what he wants the threat to do or to quit doing—is worth the risk. There's a barking dog call and the dog is vicious . . . shoot the dog? shoot the owner? What level of force would you not be embarrassed to read about in the papers the next morning?

That said, you can never let the fear of injury stop you from engaging in a lawful and necessary Use of Force. There is no perfectly safe way to apply force to another human being. The safest pressure point can cause the threat to flinch and hit his head on a wall. People, including officers, slip and fall. The only 100% safe way to do the job is not to do it at all—but that's not why you are paid. After hours of training or pages of reading all the ways that force can be viewed as excessive or all the ways it can go wrong, or reading all the scary court cases, some officers become afraid to engage. That puts them at risk and their partners at risk and the citizens at risk. Do the job.

Control. As your control increases, force should decrease. It should take less force to control a handcuffed threat than it did to get the cuffs on in the first place. When control is achieved, when you have denied the threat the means and/or opportunity to be a threat, the Use of Force is over. Anything done after control is achieved is unnecessary, and probably assault.

Noncompliance. You can usually justify an escalation in force through the simple fact that the force you are using is not working. This is more obvious at the higher end of the force continuum. If you are engaged in a fight with a threat in an altered mental state who is trying to hurt you and focused blows are not working, you may have no choice but to resort to deadly force. If you are trying to force a threat to the ground for handcuffing, and he is not responding to any pain-compliance or unbalancing technique that may, in and of itself, justify a focused blow.

There are some caveats, however. You cannot justify an increase in force for not following instructions if the threat had no chance to follow them.

> The threat was mostly controlled but struggling as officers pushed him into the corner of an elevator. One officer, arriving late on the scene began to order the threat to, "Get down!" The poor guy couldn't. He was jammed in the corner and could barely move.

That officer could not have justifiably escalated force based on the failure to comply.

If you are going to escalate force, be sure that it is still reasonable. It is easy to get caught up in the action and escalate to win, getting your ego involved.

Be prepared. Nothing works 100% of the time, not even a bullet to the head. At all times, be prepared to change what you are doing if it doesn't work.

1.10 The Final Note

The key to a long career in dealing with violent bad guys is simple: Make good decisions, execute those decisions properly, and document it well. A good report is your friend. The report should include not only what the threat did and what you did, but why you did what you did, and how you made your decisions. Don't be afraid to write about your feelings if they influenced your decisions.

No matter what the media and the citizens sometimes seem to demand, you are human, too. You will experience fights and you will be scared and angry, and, sometimes, weirdly elated. That's all normal.

Make good decisions.

In order to do this, you must know the policy and the law inside out. You must be aware of what is going on around you, but also internally. When you respond emotionally, whether with anger or fear, your judgment will be imperfect. The ability to remain detached comes with experience. There are a few officers who rely on their emotions or believe that the anger gives them an edge.

Emotional officers tend to burn out quickly. To do the job well, learn the job well.

Not knowing the job well and letting your ego get involved leads to decisions of unnecessary force. If you don't pay attention to all of your options, especially talking, it's really easy to focus on physical skills and the force options on your belt when there was another way.

Execute the decisions properly.

There is an enormous amount of information and skills you need to master to become a good cop. Make the time. Knowing what to do is not the same skill as actually doing it. To execute your decisions properly will take practice and training and confidence. The confidence will come from training and practice.

Officers without sufficient skill at low levels of force must use higher levels of force. If you can't talk a situation down and have never been able to get the take-downs and locks you learned at the academy to work, your weakness forces you to use the baton where another officer wouldn't. Develop the skills at all of your levels of force. It will take more time than you will be given for training. Do it on your own.

Document the decisions well.

You must be able to explain your decisions. In the written report after a force incident, in interviews with investigators and possibly testifying on the stand to a jury, you have to be able to explain why your decision was proper and necessary.

Articulating these decisions is a skill. In a fast, high-end use of

While in-processing to go to Iraq as a contractor, we were given a legal brief on the law of land warfare and the Rules of Engagement. The young lawyer who gave the talk said that different districts might have different rules, "For instance," he said, "in some areas the commanders have decreed that you can only use force to defend yourself, or coalition forces, not natives." I caught him later, and asked if that meant that if I saw a terrorist shooting up an Iraqi orphanage, I couldn't fire on him. He said, "Not legally." That was a glitch for me. Screw that. If it comes up, they can charge me. I'd rather be tried as a war criminal, than live with doing nothing while children were murdered.

force, you will make most of your decisions subconsciously. You must practice reconstructing what your subconscious noticed so that you can explain it in words.

Then you have to choose the words. Avoid jargon. The jury that may evaluate your actions won't know what "1234" means and will assume that A/H stands for Asshole and not Aggressive/Hostile. Without using the words "Intent, Means, and Opportunity," every single one of those elements has to be so clear in the report that the reader sees and feels them just like you did. Explain, explicitly, why you used the force that you did and why it was the lowest level of force that would have worked safely.

The last thing—this section is theoretical. It is all true and at the same time, it is all bullshit. A high-end ugly use of force can go from nothing to deadly, to over in the space of a breath. There is no one who consciously weighs all of these factors and makes conscious decisions.

Trust yourself. Read the policy and law. If something glitches, if it feels wrong, work it out in advance. Internalize your ethics. Even surprised and scared, you will stick to your ethical core. Make it strong and something to be proud of and you will be fine.

Course Objectives
Use of Cover
FORCE CONTINUUM
Hadar
Hadar
Hadar

SECTION 2: NEITHER HERE NOR THERE

If you have paid attention to this point, you should know what a rookie officer knows about force policy and law. You also know it very much the way a rookie does, as words on paper and ideas in your head. Now, go out and apply it in the real world. Better yet, don't. There are a few other things you might want to know.

Most rookies are given a very brief introduction to what could happen if they don't follow force policy. You deserve a bit more than that. So do they, but an Internal Affairs investigation is one of those things that we hope the rookie will never need to know.

Rookies at the academy are also taught some specific skills for using force—approved restraint and control tactics, and how to use firearms, OC, batons, and Tasers.

Lastly, for civilians who might need to use force, a quick overview of force law might be valuable. I'm sure my publisher will put this warning at the front of the book, but I'll echo here. This section is a guideline and not to be taken as legal advice. I am not a lawyer.

2.1 Checks and Balances

What happens when a Use of Force is suspected of being bad? It will be handled either through an internal process, or investigated by another agency.

This is the flow of events:

1. Officer is involved in an incident.
2. Someone—the threat, a witness, a fellow officer—decides that there was something wrong with the officer's actions.
3. The suspicion of wrongdoing is reported to another officer, a supervisor, a hot line, the Internal Affairs office, the press, the District Attorney, the chief . . .

4. Whoever receives the initial report turns the information over to the people it should have been reported to, usually Internal Affairs (IA).
5. IA decides whether it warrants investigation and at what level.
6. An investigation is conducted.
7. A finding is reached.
8. The officer is disciplined or isn't.

Most of the book is about point one above. Again, aspects of the reality of this will be discussed in section three, "Experience." Here, "Checks and Balances," is about the way things are supposed to happen.

The Complainant. Someone decides there was something wrong with the officer's actions. Who that someone is, what they believed was wrong, and how they perceived it all weigh on how the complaint will be investigated.

When the complainant has something to gain, for instance, they are the threat or might be related to the threat, or have personal history with the person they are making the complaint about, that is extremely relevant.

> The woman being booked for DUII (Driving Under the Influence of Intoxicants) wanted to talk to a supervisor. That was me. She claimed that my officers had raped her during the ten minutes she had been in booking.
>
> I offered to check the video immediately.
>
> "There are cameras? Wait, I remember. It happened outside."
>
> My officers hadn't gone outside the building that night and wore a different color uniform than the road officers—but I offered to check those cameras, too.
>
> She then decided it was the arresting officers, on the way to booking; they had stopped the car and . . .
>
> I told her that the arresting officers had called in to dispatch when they began the transport, and again on their arrival here. A discrepancy of even a minute would help corroborate her story. I also told her that I had already notified detectives, and they were

on the way. Whether her story had already fallen apart or not, it was an accusation of a major crime, and would be investigated.

One of the reasons for the cameras, and a primary reason for the policy to call in to dispatch at the beginning and end of transports, is that it is common for some arrestees to make allegations of serious crime, or abuse, and then offer to drop the complaint in exchange for the officers dropping the charges.

An *uninvolved citizen* is usually objective (that does not mean unemotional) about what they observed, but may not have the experience to know what is or is not an appropriate use of force. Objective does not necessarily mean calm or rational. Watching force can be traumatic. Some studies have indicated that witnessing an incident of bullying can be more traumatic to bystanders than it was to the victim.* Many citizens feel a need to do *something* about an incident that strikes them as so wrong . . . and any use of force or violence will strike certain good, peaceful people as wrong on a gut level, no matter how justified it was.

An officer who makes a complaint against another officer is taken very seriously. Unless the two officers have history. An agency can be very much like a small town, where everybody knows far too much about each other. Political and personal battles are often fought with formal and informal complaints, much like any other office.

None of this means that the complaints are dismissed out-of-hand. An uninvestigated complaint gives the appearance of a cover-up, and agencies are very sensitive to giving the slightest hint of the breath of the possibility of a cover-up.

A complainant with an obvious agenda, however, can make it simple to disprove the accusation, often without opening a full investigation or removing an officer from duty.

The Complaint. When a complaint comes in, the person receiving it records the relevant details—*who, where, when,* and as accurately as possible, *what* happened. The recipient also records who

* Rivers, et al. "Observing Bullying at School: The Mental Health Implications," *School Psychology Quarterly* vol. 24 no.4 (2009) American Psychological Association.

made the complaint and gets contact information for follow-up by the investigators.

It is very common for a citizen to make a complaint about a use of force that was completely within policy. Most citizens have very little experience with force (this is good, it means we are doing our jobs) and any use of force can appear shocking to an inexperienced observer. A complaint of this nature is taken very politely, but if what the complainant describes does not amount to a violation, it will not be investigated, no matter how shocked the citizen claims to be.

Lastly—and I should save this for the 'experience' section but I don't want to sound too harsh here: If you call and make a complaint and I call you a few days later to follow up and you don't remember the fake name that you used to make the complaint, I will, being human, be somewhat skeptical of your complaint.

Kicking It Up. Whoever gets the original complaint has a responsibility. It will vary by agency: In some, if the complaint seems minor, a supervisor can give a verbal reprimand or some on-the-spot-training. Otherwise, the complaint is either forwarded directly to Internal Affairs (IA) or kicked up the chain of command to IA.

If a complaint is made and not forwarded properly, anyone who should have forwarded it is liable for discipline. Agencies are very sensitive about accusations of a cover-up. In many agencies, not reporting a minor violation is a major violation.

Assessment. Internal Affairs will go over the substance of the complaint—and decide one of four things:

1) On the surface, the complaint is obviously false: the Internal Affairs Unit will usually send a polite letter to the complainant but will not investigate. For instance, when someone alleges a wrongful use of force on a date and time the officer in question was in court, or someone complains about an officer who retired years ago.
2) The complaint does not describe something that would constitute a violation. Most citizens know very little about laws pertaining to force and much less about policy. Often, when the complainant describes exactly what he or she saw, it is clear that the

officer's behavior was lawful and within policy. The complainant will receive a polite letter. No investigation will be conducted.

3) If the allegation is credible—or at least not obviously false—and the actions described would constitute a policy violation, Internal Affairs will investigate.
4) If the allegation is credible and rises to the level of a crime, it will normally be forwarded to another agency for criminal investigation. The Internal Affairs Unit may conduct a parallel investigation, primarily focused on policy violations. This is an administrative investigation and is not considered double jeopardy.

When parallel internal and criminal investigations are conducted, there can be some complicated legal issues, e.g., an employee can be disciplined for not cooperating with an internal investigation. If that information is then available to the criminal investigation, it may be considered coerced. It is common, as a safeguard, for the IA investigation to be put 'on hold' until the criminal investigation is concluded.

Investigation. Internal Affairs or another agency will then conduct a thorough investigation. It will differ from a standard criminal investigation because the investigating authority (Internal Affairs Unit) or the accuser, in the case of a criminal investigation, is also the suspect's employers. For that reason, officers investigated get all the protections of both a criminal defendant and a represented employee under current labor law. This is why agencies are seldom willing to discuss cases and seem to favor officers by making sure that they have legal and union representation before questioning or sometimes when writing reports on major incidents. It is not because of some "code of silence" but simply because they can be accused of labor law violations for discussing disciplinary, or potential disciplinary, action.

If criminal charges are preferred, the agencies might be somewhat more forthcoming.

The Finding. Criminal investigations of officers are handled like any other criminal investigation—and will end like any other criminal investigation, with a finding of guilt or innocence from a jury, a plea bargain, or the District Attorney deciding not to press charges. Often, there will be a concurrent IA investigation. It is possible, even common, for an officer to not be found guilty or not tried for a criminal offense, and still be sanctioned for a violation of policy. This is not double jeopardy.

IA findings will be exonerated, unfounded, unsustained, or sustained.

Exonerated means that the officer acted appropriately. If the complaint alleged, for instance, an excessive use of force, the investigators will review video if available, read reports, and question witnesses. If, at the end of the investigations it is proven that the force used was proper for the level of threat the officer perceived, the finding is *exonerated.*

Unfounded means that the investigators were able to disprove the complaint. It sometimes takes a lot of digging, but frequently, the initial allegation is shown to be false.

Unsustained means that there was insufficient evidence to prove guilt or innocence. Effectively, "exonerated" and "unfounded" are findings of innocence. Unsustained is more a finding of "not guilty."

Sustained means that the officer was found to be in violation. The officer will be sanctioned.

Sanctions. If the findings are exonerated, unfounded, or unsustained, there will be no punishment. If the complaint is sustained, the officer will be given a punishment ranging from a verbal reprimand to getting fired. The officer will have a right to appeal determined by his contract and state labor law.

Civilian Review Boards. Many agencies have implemented Civilian Review Boards (CRBs). These are panels of civilians who are a sort of double-check on the Internal Affairs process.

Officers are involved in many force situations nationwide, every day. Most go unquestioned. Those few that are questioned are usually handled internally, by IA. In most cases, the officers are cleared.

Some incidents, however, get a lot of public scrutiny. In those cases, again, the officer is usually cleared. Sometimes citizens are outraged, and it does have the appearance of friends investigating friends, or the fox guarding the henhouse—seriously, cops investigating cops?

So citizens call for and politicians empower CRBs to check IA's work. In some areas, the CRB works from the IA investigation and documents. In others, the CRB is empowered to conduct its own investigation.

When CRBs are started, there is usually a huge outcry from the police unions: That a CRB will lead to witch hunts, that only people who hate the police will apply for the positions, that the CRB exists solely to punish officers who have already been cleared. Even the calmer heads are worried having seen how little most citizens really know about violence and crime. How can a panel of civilians effectively evaluate what an officer does? Do patients investigate medical malpractice? Do passengers investigate airplane crashes?

In real life, CRBs have done very little to rock the boat. Both CRBs and IA units give "sustained" findings only about 10-15% of the time.* The simple fact is that before they can evaluate an officer's conduct, they need to be trained on policy and law. After such training, they tend to make the same determination that IA did. Again, most officers are cleared most of the time.

Some people will not be happy with it, but that is what tends to happen when you educate people: they learn to recognize a good decision.

2.2 Skills Taught at the Academy

There are state, regional, and federal academies throughout the United States. Some municipalities run their own academy separate from the state academies—sometimes to save money, often to deliver skills that more closely match their needs.

States have set standards for the minimum training for new police officers. Some states have set additional standards for continuing training. Some haven't. According to a Bureau of Justice Statistics paper from 1997, seven of eight agencies required annual training. Bureau of Justice Statistics "Local Police Departments, 1997," October 1999.

Many competing interests affect what is taught to recruits. Money

* John Chasnoff, "A Review of Civilian Review," *Synthesis/Regeneration,* vol. 39 Winter 2006.

> At one level, law enforcement is about crime prevention, protecting the citizens, and customer service—solving problems. At another level, it is about budgets, bureaucracy, politics, and perception. Neither of these is the 'right' way. An agency that fails at either level has failed.
>
> It becomes troubling, even poisonous, when these two values are separated in the agency, and fighting against each other . . . when the people working the streets or the people in the office come to believe that the other group is somehow the enemy.

is one of the most powerful. Training is expensive and takes time. Time is money, in this instance, because the officer being trained must be paid, his instructors must be paid, and training equipment must be bought. An officer in training is not patrolling and another officer must be paid, probably at overtime rates, to cover.

This puts administrators under incredible pressure to limit training. Administrations are often measured on how they handle the budget, and good training can put a hell of a dent in a budget.

This is offset by another fear of another cost—liability. Good training is one of the most effective ways to prevent bad decisions. When you limit training to save money, you risk an increase in bad decisions, each of which might result in very expensive lawsuits.

Very few of the senior leaders of law enforcement agencies, with the exception of County Sheriffs, are elected. But almost universally, the people who appointed them are. This requires a political creature who can manage the media and public perception. This is not a value judgment—a "good man" who understands the troops and local crime but has no rapport with the media, or can't function in the political arena, is nearly useless.

Cost. Liability. Political pressure. Public perception. And, finally, the skills that the officer needs to do the job. Somewhere in the balance of these competing interests, each academy and each agency that conducts continuing training decides on a curriculum. There are things that must be included in classes—how to write reports, protect evidence, laws that pertain to police operations, first aid, EVOC (Emergency Vehicle Operations Course) . . .

The physical skills of force present interesting problems. Force use has a very high risk of liability, and training can be slanted for or against liability protection versus effectiveness.

A system of defensive tactics, for instance, that promises to restrain threats without injuring them is very appealing from a liability standpoint. Uninjured threats sue less often and for smaller amounts. It sounds good. Unfortunately, such systems may not work.

Training in physical skills works better the more closely it matches the real force environment. The more closely training looks like a 'real fight,' however, the higher the injury rate in training. Training injuries can be expensive in many ways—wage replacement, medical bills, overtime to cover the injured officer's shifts, and potential liability.

This makes it very easy for training authorities to justify minimal training in hands-on skills.

Then, from the street side—you use verbal skills most often, low-level force next, and lethal force rarely or never in a normal career. It seems to make sense to concentrate training on the skills you use the

Full disclosure here: When I talk about street level opinion or the view from the streets, I'm talking about the views of the best, most active officers (see section 3.1).

Officers are people, and people have an unbelievable ability to manage their own reality. Officers who avoid trouble convince themselves that trouble is rare. The same officer may also find Defensive Tactics training sweaty, uncomfortable, and potentially embarrassing or painful. They can often come up with many reasons about why something they dislike doing is unnecessary to do. It is human nature.

It works the other way, too. It is much more rare than it is presented in film, but there are officers who live in a fantasy world where they imagine themselves the heroes in a dark and violent world. You can sometimes pick them out because they try to get high-end training, but don't work that hard at the basic skills. They are too cool for that.

most. Unfortunately, the risk of injury and the potential stakes run in the exact opposite order. Should you train in the thing you use 95% of the time? Or in the things you use rarely but where failure equals death? Your answer to that tends to depend on whether it is your death under discussion.

What skills pertaining to force are actually taught at an academy? It differs by jurisdiction. Generally,

Use of Force

The rookies will be given an introduction to policy and law that is very much like section one of this book. Some academies teach Use of Force in conjunction with force options, particularly Defensive Tactics. That is a good thing. It is easy to separate the physical skills from the legal requirements and that is rarely beneficial. All of the physical skills, at all levels, should be trained in conjunction with the judgment required to choose an appropriate force option.

> Teaching to the 2's. One of my friends at the academy explained the philosophy of "teaching to the 2's." Ranking recruits on a scale of 1-10, the 2's are the lowest common denominator of students.
>
> An academy trainer said, "We don't have any say in what recruits we get. Some of them, the 2's, are completely unfit for the job. We have a responsibility to teach them what we can, so we dumb it down so that the lowest common denominator has a chance."
>
> I disagree. If someone has made it to early adulthood and is still in the bottom 20%, that's either a disability or a lifestyle choice. In either case, training won't matter much. By "teaching to the 2's," effort is aimed at people who won't improve, and the good people are bored out of the learning cycle.
>
> I also wonder what business a person who is in the bottom 20% has choosing a job where they may have to make split-second life-or-death decisions.

Defensive Tactics

This is often the catch-all term for unarmed skills ranging from handcuffing to survival fighting. Some academies include all non-firearm force skills under this label. Some include it under Use of Force. In many cases, the rookie graduates from the academy and goes on the street with as little as forty hours of training. Many officers feel that academy training places a higher emphasis on liability reduction (fewer injuries in training, fewer potential injuries to the threat) than on effectiveness.

Firearms

Most academies spend a significant amount of time on firearms training. Though guns are the force option least likely to be used, they are the option with the greatest stakes and the greatest liability. That said, marksmanship requirements are not that high to graduate from many academies. A typical course of qualification might include:

- Stage 1: Starting from the 25-yard-line the cadet has seventy-five seconds to draw and fire six rounds from the prone position, three rounds strong hand* kneeling, six rounds strong side standing, and three rounds weak side kneeling.
- Stage 2: From fifteen yards, the cadet will draw and fire two rounds in six seconds, lower the weapon, then fire four sets of two rounds. The cadet is allowed three seconds for each double tap.
- Stage 3: From the seven-yard line, the cadet draws and fires 12 rounds in fifteen seconds with one mandatory reload.
- Stage 4: From the five-yard line, the cadet draws and fires five rounds with the strong hand, reloads and fires five with the weak hand.

This is a generic range. More progressive agencies** and academies have researched officer-involved shootings, and designed the training and qualification around real experience.

* If 'strong' or 'weak' hand is specified, it indicates one-handed shooting. If not specified, the shooter fires from a two-handed grip.

** I'm being judgmental, but it disturbs me that this particular course shoots in multiples of six. That indicates that they haven't re-evaluated their standards since they gave up revolvers.

Baton, OC, and Taser

Most academies include training in baton (either regular, side-handle, or expandable) and OC, as they are common in most agencies. Taser training, as the 'new kid on the block' is largely left up to the agencies. In a tight training schedule, there is little point in training all new recruits in a tool that is only supported, supplied, and authorized by some of their agencies.

Baton and OC training run as briefly as four hours for each, rarely as long as sixteen. With OC, much of that time is classroom training covering propellants, and spray patterns and history and other things that are easy to test but irrelevant in the field. Taser training is similar.

Confrontational Simulations (ConSim)

ConSim, or scenario training, puts the rookie officer in situations with role players that they must treat, as much as possible, like real life. Properly trained and equipped, a ConSim allows the officer the full range of force options (Simunition weapons are fully functioning firearms that fire sub-caliber marking rounds); foam batons, training Tasers, OC and armored role-players with all of force policy and law in effect.

It requires the rookie to develop physical skills in tandem with judgment. It simulates the chaos of a real force situation, and also allows and rewards non-force solutions, when applicable. It's great training. It's also somewhat dangerous (the more closely anything matches real life, the more likely there will be injuries) and very expensive, requiring specialized equipment, ammunition, role-players, safety officers and a facilitator.

Because of the expense, not all agencies and academies use scenario training but most rookies find it an invaluable taste of real life.

According to A Bureau of Justice Statistics Special Report on academies nationwide (February 2009 NCJ 222987), the average academy teaches:

Self Defense[*] 51 hours
Firearms 60 hours
Non-lethal[**] weapons 12 hours

Not much, is it? Simulation training, if they have it, will come out of these hours. So will training on policy and law pertaining to force. Nationally, basic recruit training averages 761 hours, roughly a 19-week course.

2.3 Force Law for Civilians

As mentioned, force laws for officers and civilians are very similar at the basic level. Remember, I am not a lawyer. Do not construe this as legal advice.

Each state is different. You need to know your specific state law thoroughly and examine it for requirements and exceptions. Still, you use the minimum force you need to safely resolve the situation.

Where an officer might be required to intervene, this is generally not true for civilians. Both officers and civilians must be able to articulate that the threat had Intent, Means, and Opportunity. The civilian, however, must also be able to articulate Preclusion. Preclusion means that there was nothing other than force that would have worked. In other words, leaving was not an option. Calling for help would not have worked or would not have worked in time. The citizen has to show that *there was no choice other than force.*

"Self-defense" is an *affirmative defense.* If you are accused of a crime, say assault or homicide, and you assert self-defense, you are admitting to the basic facts of assault or murder. You are acknowledging that you did beat or kill the other person. As an affirmative defense, it is then on you to prove that you had no choice. An affirmative defense shifts the burden of proof from the prosecution to the defense. Your ability to articulate and prove preclusion is critical.

* This is the term that Bureau of Justice Statistics (BJS) uses and probably includes everything from survival fighting to handcuffing a compliant arrest.

** Another BJS term. There is no such thing as a "non-lethal" weapon. People have been killed with pillows. Most agencies in my experience use the term "Less-lethal" to denote things like pepper spray, batons, beanbag rounds, and Tasers.

This is modified in several jurisdictions. If your state has a duty to retreat clause built into the self-defense laws, you may be required to exhaust all possible means of escape before defending yourself physically.

If your state has a "stand your ground law," as long as you have a legal right to be in a place and are not doing anything illegal in that place, you have no duty to retreat or find another option, whatsoever. Stand your ground laws, on the surface, appear to remove the need for articulating 'preclusion.' So it seems. I'd hate to be the test case.

Castle laws are more common. They generally state that if someone illegally enters your home (or place of business, or vehicle in some jurisdictions), you have largely unfettered right to self-defense. Basically, preclusion is no longer a concern and Intent, Means, and Opportunity are considered manifest in the invasion of your home.

That is a layman's thumbnail sketch. Check your state statutes for yourself and if you need to, consult a lawyer. This is not a subject for amateurs.

As complex as that may seem, it only applies to defending yourself or another person. Be very, very careful in defending property. The rules are usually far stricter. Using force, particularly lethal force, to prevent theft or destruction of property is much harder to justify than to prevent harm. It is even harder if it is not your property.

SECTION 3: EXPERIENCE

HARD TRUTH #8

Experience will change you.

Maybe that doesn't seem like a hard truth to you. Often, it isn't. Growth and learning are just change. The longer you live, the more experience, the greater the change. In theory. It is a hard truth when it is based on hard experience.

The more intense the things you are exposed to, the less power normal experience will seem to have. Scraping a knee is a big deal for a toddler; not worth noticing to a boxer; trivial to the survivor of a bad car accident.

There are ways to manage the exposure, but an officer's day-to-day job is to deal with very intense situations. Have you ever been pulled-over and been given a ticket? Do you remember the feeling in your stomach? The officer felt that too, the first time . . . maybe the first hundred.

The side effect is that the individual's reasons why he had to speed and why the law should not apply in this one particular case are things the officer has heard many, many times before. This emotional event in the life of the speeder is only a routine and possibly aggravating aspect of the officer's workday.

Most people reading this have never seen a truly shattered corpse. Some have never seen a corpse at all . . . you pull a couple out of wrecks, and that is the context in which you hear the excuses and rationalizations. The excuses start to sound like bullshit, especially when you know damn well that every cry for greater sympathy from officers is, in the end, a self-serving cry for the rules not to apply to that person. That's a hard truth too, but since it's not about force and reactions to force, it doesn't get its own nifty label.

3.1 Types of Officers

To be fair, not all officers will have the same levels of experience. Not all will do the job with equal skill. When we talk about how experience changes officers, you have to take that into account. There are different kinds of officers and they tend to have experiences and attitudes that match their level.

Generally, officers start as eager rookies. Then they will become Lops, average officers, meat-eaters, posers, and/or burnouts.

Eager Rookie

The eager rookie wants to learn everything he can. He or she is often terrified of making a mistake and tends to stick to the rules, as well as they remember them. That is a key—a more experienced officer who understands the rules has more confidence in his or her discretionary power. A rookie will rarely cut slack because they have no real idea when it is appropriate, or even safe, to do so.

Robbie's spent the last 6 months in the academy and the staff tells him he's ready to hit the street. If he wasn't at the top of the class, it wasn't because he wasn't trying. He knows he's going to be part of The Thin Blue Line . . . and he's pretty sure he's ready. He's motivated, idealistic, and ready to save the world.

But Robbie is a rookie. The academy taught him all the book stuff, and the scenarios there gave him a taste of the job—but he's starting to see why his Field Training Officer says that he is barely ready to do the job. He's constantly being tested by new situations, by his supervisors, and by his coworkers. He's energetic, motivated . . . and he's just starting to feel like an officer.

There is also a lot to learn for a rookie—they must memorize the geography of their district; drive while handling the radio and the MDT (Mobile Data Terminal); and familiarize themselves with both criminal laws and the procedural laws of evidence and with the big book of policy and procedure.

It's a lot to learn and it is learned in a context of very high stakes.

A mistake in procedure could allow a violent felon to walk free. A mistake in decision-making during a force incident can result in injury or death to a suspect, a suspect who may not be guilty of anything. Fear of making that mistake can make a rookie or even an experienced officer hold back and end with the officer's death.

The kind of officer the rookie will become will depend on his character, his early experiences, and the officers that he takes as role models early in his career.

The Lop

(I have no idea why they are called 'Lops' or if it is merely a local term—other areas call them ROAD officers, Retired On Active Duty) is best described as a civil servant with a strong union. Every large agency has them. Secure in the knowledge that they can't be fired under any but the most extraordinary circumstances, they will do the minimum required and no more.

> The lieutenant doesn't like the new guy on the shift. He's popular with the other troops and always seems to be first there when something goes bad. The new officer is a show-off and a cowboy. The lieutenant has decided to fix him, because it is a lieutenant's job to be in charge and point out and fix errors.
>
> The lieutenant kicks back a report for a rewrite, like he does every time for this officer. It's not a terrible report, and the lieutenant knows that this officer teaches report writing, but the officer needs to learn who is in charge.
>
> The next day, the officer turns in the re-written report. The lieutenant glances over it.
>
> "Good. That's hundred percent better," the lieutenant says, never noticing that not a single word has been changed.

The Lop often gains very little experience. There is a skill to avoiding the stresses at work. It can be as simple as just being slow to answer the radio. Be a little slow, take a wrong turn or two, and an eager rookie or a pro will get there first and take care of the most dangerous

> Does that sound cynical, that administrators were sometimes inferior officers? It is a sad thing, but true. They never believe it, however. I have heard administrators, widely regarded as cowards by their former partners, brag that they had never had to draw their weapon because of their superior verbal skills, when the simple fact was that they avoided any situation risky enough that a weapon would have been required. I have heard senior administrators explicitly state that a man was promoted because he wasn't safe to be on the streets.
>
> If you ever wonder why a poll of police administrators often gives attitudes and beliefs diametrically opposed to the beliefs and attitudes of line officers, this is one of the reasons.

seconds of the call. The smarter Lops lobby for desk jobs or to be assigned to a quiet patrol district. The very smart ones will use those assignments and the exposure to supervisors that a desk job provides, to work their way into administration and off the streets entirely.

The end result is that in a few large agencies, the upper management is composed almost entirely of people who were inferior officers. They write policy and make decisions based on the job the way that they experienced it—behind a desk or hiding from danger.

This is a common complaint, too, that I have heard from the West Coast of the United States to the North East border of Iraq.

Average Joes

Most officers are just guys. *Average Joes.*

> Steve is a big, burly guy with a ferocious laugh and a gentle nature. He's not bad to have around in a fight, and other officers come to him when they want to talk. He's been a tactical operator, but it was more about the camaraderie of the team than some thirst for adventure.
>
> His true love is his son, who was born with a lot of health problems. Steve worked tirelessly to be there for the baby, and to

> make sure that all expenses were covered. He loves his job and he's good at it, but Steve works to provide for his family.

They do the job. They do it well. But it is just a job. They will handle what comes up—and that can be a lot of intense experience over the years—but they will not strive to make the job harder than it is. They will kick down doors if asked or if it is necessary, but they will not volunteer for the assignments where high risk is routine. The average officer keeps the agency going. It is mentally the healthiest of the personnel profiles.

Meat Eaters

Then there are the meat-eaters. Most agencies have them and they need them. These are the men and women who volunteer for high-risk assignments, the ones who run to danger.

> It was a new team, still learning the ropes. The Corrections Division had never had a tactical team, and had no idea if their "knuckle-dragging jail guards" could show the necessary professionalism. When a psychologist asked to study them, to sit-in on trainings, the administration enthusiastically agreed. The team itself didn't seem to care one way or the other.
>
> The first part of one particular training day had been spent in serious hand-to-hand, which means the team was beating the merry living hell out of each other—and having a lot of fun doing it. Then the voice came over the loudspeaker—there was a real problem upstairs. The team was ordered to fix it.
>
> The psychologist was disturbed, honestly—even a little afraid. She had spent the morning watching the punishment the team dished-out to each other, to people that they liked. She couldn't imagine, and wasn't sure she wanted to see, what they would do to a real criminal.
>
> The team filed into the cellblock, faces masked, silent. The team leader spoke to the inmate for a few minutes. The inmate looked at the group of cold-eyed officers and decided not to

fight. The team cuffed him and took him to a disciplinary cell. Everything was done in absolute silence.

When the team got on the elevator, safely out of hearing of any inmates, they gave whoops and high-fives. The psychologist heard the team leader say, "That was a perfect operation. Nothing happened."

Not all meat-eaters have the same level of skill. A meat-eater without an appetite for extensive training and constant learning stands to have a very short career. Also, they are not equally skilled in the same arenas. Most specialize. A good CNT (Crisis Negotiation Team) are just as much meat-eaters as SWAT.

As important as it is to have people to kick down doors, and as critical as it is to have specialized skills available to deal with volatile situations, meat-eaters and Lops have a deep contempt for each other. In an agency where Lops have moved into administration, being a meat-eater is a career-ender.

Extremely active officers will also draw more complaints than inactive officers. That is simple math. An officer who makes 100 felony arrests will have at least 100 people who do not like the fact that he is doing the job. A few will complain, no matter how well the job was done or how professionally the officer acted.

Even if/when the officer is cleared of wrongdoing, the complaint may stay in his or her file or linger in the memory of supervisors.

An officer who makes no felony arrests, perhaps by staying at a desk job, will likely have no complaints in his or her file. On paper, the officer who did nothing may look like a better officer than the one who performed spectacularly.

Posers

Posers are a special case. Whether because they are packing a resume or trying to live an adolescent fantasy, these are the men and women who volunteer for the high-visibility, high-risk assignments but don't have the appetite for danger and training of the true meat-eaters. It is easier to get on a team than it is to be a valuable member.

> The officer is eager to show me his new equipment. A flashlight that strobes, an M-4 rifle with a heavy barrel and electronic equipment stuck on three rails. "I buy my own stuff. The department doesn't get the best. If my life depends on it, I want the best."
>
> His uniform is perfectly pressed, boots polished. He is upset that the department's tactical team patch isn't "subdued enough"—he would like the lighter shades of gray to be darkened.
>
> Later, over lunch with his commander, the officer's name comes up. I ask the commander how he ranks the man as an operator.
>
> "He sure dresses pretty," is all the commander will say.

Rookies and outsiders can rarely tell a poser from a meat-eater.

Burnouts

Lastly, the burnouts. This is hard to categorize, because there are many different ways to burn out. Meat-eaters often burn out when they find that their efforts and risks are largely unappreciated by their own administration. Being very active and doing dangerous jobs puts the officer under greater scrutiny and at greater liability risk. It can make a job that often seems thankless feel punishing.

> His career was stuck at sergeant. He didn't care, or didn't seem to. He'd been a shining star once: hard-working, hyper-intelligent, dedicated. That didn't seem to matter. He'd seen others who didn't work as hard move up. He was taking orders now from people who weren't good enough to wipe his boots, when they were officers. He'd held some of their hands, and wiped their noses.
>
> Didn't matter. Not anymore. He'd been grouchy for long enough that he had a good place to work—no lieutenant, most days. Not much work. A good crew, but he'd boss them around anyway. He was careful to always be sober at work.

Any officer can burn out when the intensity of experience overwhelms his or her ability to cope. The nature of the job means that you cannot predict or prepare for how much or what kinds of things will happen. Sometimes it piles on.

A shooting is stressful. A multiple fatality Motor Vehicle Accident (MVA), especially with dead children, is stressful. The suicide of a partner is hellishly stressful. Who would be prepared for all three in close succession?

And some burn out just like in any other job—through boredom and mid-life crisis and the realization that what you thought would be a fun, exciting career has become a job.

The last contributor to burnout, one of the most common, is isolation. As officers (or any emergency services professionals) see more and more intense things that other citizens (including friends and family), cannot relate to—the officer finds fewer and fewer people to simply talk to.

On Burning Out

People are formed and grow through the events in their lives. Big growth (and not all growth is positive) is spurred by big events. In normal life, being the first to get married in a group of friends changes your relationships. It changes your attitudes, your priorities, and the way you relate to life. Many friendships quietly end after a marriage, not because of a meddling spouse but because of the change in perspective.

Few things change you more than having children. If you have children, that needs no explanation. If you don't have children, no amount of explanation will make it clear. This is another area where friendships often quietly end, when one couple is the first of a group—and it quietly comes back together when other couples become parents.

These are big events—marriage and children. But they are hardly rare. There are large groups of married people and parents to form relationships and gather support. Society has systems for keeping people who go through expected change in the society.

The officer will be changed by big events, too. But his or her events, at least the ones that become 'big.' are relatively rare. Few civilians have extensive experience with violent death. A single act of violence or simple stupidity can scar an extended family as they grieve and bury someone who was too young, too full of promise, to die. An officer was there, too, almost certainly. He saw the body before it was cleaned-up and all the bits were arranged close to normal. He was the first to tell the mother, the father, the spouse . . . maybe with the aid of a chaplain or a counselor. Maybe. Without the luxury of knowing much about who they were telling and how they might react. Without the support of a family who all shared in the grief.

This single event can cripple an extended family.

The officer will have another one next week or next month or next year. Then, maybe the really bad one, with the children crushed and dead in a wrecked car, or the smell of burning flesh that you can't quite forget. In the moment, the officer has to show enough compassion to comfort and yet control feelings enough to function.

Officers live these things and they carry them. When an officer experiences something that needs to be processed, like someone trying to kill her, a friend trying to understand through the lens of a scuffle in junior high school or a martial arts movie can't relate. Even worse for the officer, sometimes, is that the civilian cannot believe or understand that they don't understand.

For many people, a bad day at work is an argument with a sales rep. For an officer, a bad day might be a trip to the ER for stitches, and a test for HEP-C and HIV.

'Slacking' in the civilian world means a project or homework isn't done on time. In law enforcement it might mean that a violent felon will continue to assault and rape . . .

A job well done might mean a good grade or a bonus or a mention at the next company meeting. For an officer, the consequences of a 'good day at work' often means a man will lose decades of freedom, locked away without access to victims (much) . . .

I could go on. Here's the point. Officers start to feel that they have little or no common ground with "ordinary citizens." It is exacerbated when there is a high-profile incident and people who know little or nothing about the circumstances, the policy, or the laws make definitive, judgmental statements. That reinforces some the officer's beliefs that the citizens are ignorant and vindictive.

That's not true. It's just some of them.

Once, on a radio call-in show a local man said, "Every time I hear about the cops, and a guy with a knife, they wind up shooting the guy. That's not right. It shouldn't happen every time." (From memory, not an exact quote.)

That's a big thing right there. Sampling error. I don't know the exact statistics, but in that jurisdiction, most knife encounters were talked down. I know of one handled with a Taser, several with pepper spray or unarmed.

Checking just one state on the Bureau of Justice Statistics site, Alabama reported 1,322 violent knife crimes. They didn't shoot anywhere near 1,322 suspects that year.

Remember section one: a knife is Means for a lethal threat. It has been shown, time and again, that a threat within 7 yards can get to an officer and stab many times before the officer can draw a sidearm. With a minimal evidence of intent (and not dropping the knife when ordered covers it), a man with a knife is a lethal threat and authorizes deadly force.

That's the classroom. In real life, officers deal with knives far more often than they shoot people.

All the shootings make the news, but where are reports of the successful talk-downs? The man was right when he said that every time

> My favorite 'basic facts are wrong' example was one speaker at a rally for a man shot by officers in Oregon. The speaker said, "That man needed an ambulance, not the police. They should have called an ambulance!"
>
> In fact, an ambulance was standing by, but refused to get within 100 yards of the threat until officers on the scene could guarantee the paramedic's safety.
>
> The threat had forced a car off the road; lost control and crashed his vehicle while attempting to do it again; was believed to have a firearm; and had then prowled through a residential district, howling and stripping off his clothes.

he *heard* about a knife-wielding threat, the officers shot. Because all the ones he knew about resulted in shootings, he believed that they all did, never questioning why he heard about it in the first place.

Officers fall into the same trap—often, when there is a shooting or other in-custody death, there will be people getting on the news and making pronouncements. Often, their most basic facts are wrong. Because these are the ones who make the news—loud, strident, bitter, critical—these are the citizens the officers see. It's an easy trap to fall into, to believe that these are the average citizens.

3.2 Concrete Thinkers: The Dilemma

One of the hardest things to explain to civilians is that there are no perfect answers in a use of force. Violence is a problem, and we have all been trained that problems have solutions. A bridge constructed in a certain way of certain materials will hold a certain amount of weight. One plus one equals two. There is a shortest route between two cities.

In medicine, perhaps, this gets fuzziest, because while there may well be an optimal treatment, not everything works the same way, every time. Different people respond to the same treatment in different ways.

I would argue that violence is more complex than medicine. In medicine, you have one body, one mind to address. In violence, there are always at least two. Medicine has a well-defined baseline for what is healthy, Within Normal Limits (WNL). By the time things escalate to violence, the person, at least mentally, is beyond the normal limits.

We know that these levels of anger, fear, or drugs affect the mind and body, but we don't know how much, or how universally. In the short time (a fraction of a second or hours) that the officer has to gather information, he can rarely tell if emotion, drugs, mental illness or just simple meanness is driving the behavior . . . and each of those would affect the mind and body differently.

The doctor works in a clinical setting with a patient who is actively cooperating in finding a diagnosis and a treatment. They work together, the patient and the doctor, in an environment designed to limit distractions and with access to incredible technology.

The officer has to make a decision about force with only the information he can gather in the time that the threat allows. It's often in poorly lit, distracting, and dangerous environments using just his own senses, experience, intelligence, and intuition with a subject who may be actively preventing the officer from getting relevant facts.

Just like a doctor, however, the price for a mistake can be a life. Unlike a doctor, the life may well be the officer's.

With all of these variables, there will never be a perfect answer. There is just stuff that worked—or didn't. And the definition of working may not be what you expect.

There are people who don't adapt well to this mental environment. This is the job: you have to make decisions. You will never have enough information to be sure you are right. Some of your decisions may leave a corpse, orphans, widows—even if the decision is good. You will never be sure. Will you take the job? If not you, who will?

> One supervisor at a local agency observed us putting several deputies through scenarios. After a particular scenario, he was appalled because two different deputies had handled the same scenario differently, and both, according to the instructors, were right. There can't be two ways to be right, he insisted.
>
> He's going to have a very tough time supervising this job.

> If you see a story about a Use of Force in the media and ask an officer whether it was 'good' he or she will almost certainly answer, "I don't know. I wasn't there."
>
> It doesn't take much experience with extremely chaotic events to realize that a decision made in a fraction of a second will be based on what you see. The officer in the media may have perceived more or less than another officer you ask. May have noticed or made connections that another officer would have missed, or may have missed something another officer would have seen.
>
> That flash, where one officer sees the hand coming up in a snappy salute and a second officer is puzzled because it was a left hand salute (and that isn't regulation), and a third officer sees the free hand slip to the holster determines, sometimes, who lives and who dies.

No two people see the same thing. Write down a description of your car and then ask your significant other to do the same. There will be differences.

Read a section of this book out loud to two friends and ask them each to write a summary. Compare the summaries. There will be differences.

If no two people perceive the same or understand quite the same, what are the odds that they will decide or act the same?

Training is important to bring some standardization to this process. Every officer should be in the ballpark of what an officer with similar experience would do, but they will not do the same thing in quite the same way.

It is even hard to measure how right a decision was. It is tempting to measure the success purely by results, but there is a fatal flaw there.

Sometimes you can do everything wrong and come out smelling like a rose. Take a TV scenario—the threat is holding a hostage, with a gun to the love interest's head. The officer, the hero of this show, has his weapon out, pointing at the threat. The threat tells him to put the weapon down. He hesitates, building up tension, and then complies.

In the movies, the hero then disarms the bad guy through some ruse or amazing martial arts skill; or, he stands there while the threat retreats, setting up a big chase scene.

In real life? The threat shoots the unarmed officer and then the hostage.

Because it worked on TV does not indicate it will work in real life. More importantly, because it worked in real life once is no indication it will work again.

There is a particularly stupid thing that I do. When an inmate is going off in a cell, screaming threats and sometimes, stripping and spitting blood, I go into the cell and talk to them. This has been spectacularly successful for me. If I saw another officer do it, I would chew him out. Here's the thing—I have been working in this area, this jail, for almost two decades. The inmates know me and I know them. They trust me to keep my word and to listen. They also know that if it gets physical, I will not hesitate.

I have an extraordinary amount of training and experience in very close-range fighting and I trust my instincts absolutely. I have a much better chance of prevailing if things go bad than most officers have.

I have no ego in this. If I don't know the inmate or if I get a bad vibe, I don't take the chance. No one will say I 'chickened out,' and I wouldn't care if anyone did.

I am very, very good at talking to crazy people and people in crisis. Actually, I'm very good at listening to them. That's the key.

Measured by results alone, this is a good tactic. When something is handled by talking, there is no injury, not to the threat, not to the officer, and not to any bystanders.

But the results come from a mix of the officer, the threat, the environment, and the particular situation. Change one thing in this equation and it has the chance to go very, very badly. So, realistically, can we set this as an operating standard? If we required officers to attempt this, some officers and many threats would be injured. More agencies have gone the other way, forbidding certain tactics that they consider high-risk.

Statistics show that under stress, even at close range, most people miss.* Skills degrade when you are afraid or surprised. Realistically, I have met two people who, under stress, could shoot a gun out of another man's hand. Two. How could we hold all officers to this standard?

With an absolute best answer not a realistic possibility, what do we have left? The Three Golden Rules, and "good enough." You and

> I think faith is the ability to *let go*. To not need to know the outcome before acting. People are risk adverse—they don't like losing, they don't like taking chances if there's a chance of loss. They like comfort and security.
>
> One of the reasons most people can't do (or even really understand) emergency services jobs is this level of faith—how much information would you need before gambling your life on a decision? For us, it seems completely logical: "As much as I can in the time I have, then roll."

* An analysis of New York Police Department shootings, 1994-2000, showed that at distances of six feet or less, trained officers missed 62% of the time.

your partner go home healthy; the bad guys you ran into wound up in jail, or at least didn't hurt anybody; and you didn't get sued; it's a good day. It's good enough.

You don't see everything coming, and there's no guarantee that you will act correctly, even if you do:

> I lived through a "teachable moment" that might tie in both the "gender" and "mental state" sections . . . maybe a couple of others, as well:
>
> While assigned to patrol in a rural region of upstate New York, I responded to a 911 dispatch of a "boyfriend/girlfriend domestic with injuries," in a stand-alone trailer.
>
> Given the geography, and limited patrol staffing, my nearest backup was a county sheriff's deputy, about 20 minutes behind me. I arrived, checked around the trailer, listened at the door for a minute, and knocked. No answer, but the door wasn't locked. I walked in to find the boyfriend sitting—calmly, quietly, and drunk—on the living room couch.
>
> His hands, face, and clothes were smeared with blood. None of it appeared to be his. I drew my sidearm, and asked him where his girlfriend was. He pointed into the kitchen, which was partially visible from my position. Rather than cuff him, as I should have, I merely told him to "sit tight," while I checked out his girlfriend.
>
> "Sure thing, trooper. I don't have a car, and I'm too shit-faced to walk anywhere."
>
> At the time, I thought that was a pretty funny line. The kitchen was empty. More blood smeared on the counter, the fridge, and a cabinet. What looked like a wooden cutting board was in the sink, blood on it, as well. And a bloody trail, leading from the kitchen to a door, down a short hallway.
>
> I found the girlfriend in the tub, alive and beaten. Bleeding a bit from nose and scalp, she had a couple of broken fingernails, she said it hurt to breathe. The boyfriend had slapped her around, then grabbed the cutting board, and went to town. She said she'd sign the complaint.

I told her to sit in the kitchen . . . I'd be back with the first aid kit, and EMS is on the way.

As I'm cuffing the boyfriend, EMS shows up. I walk to the door with the boyfriend (who has remained calm, even friendly), then feel something smack/push me between the shoulder blades. When I turn around, the Emergency Medical Technician (EMT) says, "Fuck."

I have a steak knife—a cheap, fucking, serrated steak knife with one of those cheesy, brown, plastic handles—sticking out of my back. She stabbed me with enough force to break off the plastic handle; my quartermaster told me later the point penetrated 15 of 21 layers of Kevlar. In the time it took for me to take the boyfriend by the arm, and walk the 10 or so steps to the front door—maybe five or six seconds?—the victim managed to stand up from the kitchen table, grab a knife from the dish rack, walk about 12 feet, and jab me with it. And she was stealthy—on some predatory, "Wild Kingdom" level, there was intent.

Jesus, was I pissed—at the absurdity of it all, as much as the girl. Ten minutes or so earlier, boyfriend had been beating her to a pulp with a cutting board, to the point where she had to lock herself in the bathroom, and cower in a bathtub, like an abused pet. But as soon as she saw me taking "the love of her life" out the door in cuffs, I stopped being a human being/white knight/public servant, and instead, became "the enemy" to her. And not even with the dignity of unique offense, but in that abstract, detached way just about all Law Enforcement Officers (LEOs) are painted.

Lessons? 1) Don't take it personally when someone takes a shot at you. Sure, when I was in basic at the academy, my street survival and firearms instructors alluded to this, but there was always an undercurrent of job-induced bravado . . . rather like, "If anyone DARES to bring it, make them sorry they ever even THOUGHT about doing it." It's tempting . . . ohhh, it is so tempting . . . but ultimately, it's unprofessional.

3.3 Dark Moments: Will You Act?

We always watch rookies, especially their response to their first fight, or high-risk situation. Some run to it. Some run away. Some freeze. Until that first fight, we don't know what the rookie will do. Neither does the rookie. I have supervised a tiny, single mom with no experience in this field, and no martial arts training, who jumped on a huge inmate to stop a fight. When the inmate threw her across the room, she jumped on him again. In the same week, a 6'4" former marine was verbally challenged by an inmate. The former marine ran and hid.

We don't know, and we haven't found anything that reliably predicts, who will run towards danger and who will run away. I've seen martial arts champions freeze; big, buff athletes cower; and tiny nerds turn into tigers. We can't tell, so we watch.

For some, it is empowering.

> "I think the Use of Force that really stands out, in my mind, happened just a few months after I started working at the jail. When I first got the job, I realized that I truly wanted to be the best Deputy I could possibly be. That meant for me to join a gym to start lifting weights besides getting back to running again. After a few months of lifting, I was working on the counter with Rick and Kent on a very busy Friday night, one of those 'over 100 bookings' nights. We were all three working well together as a team. I was dealing with a guy, about 25-30 yrs. old, that got a bit mouthy with me and started jerking away from me. I automatically spun the guy around and pulled his arm up behind his back, so he was practically touching the back of his head. Rick and Kent watched me take him to a sep cell.* I looked at Rick and Kent with such a huge smile on my face, and was practically jumping up and down. I had no idea that I could do that, nor that I had the strength to do that. I really wanted to tell the dirt-bag that he got 'beat' by a 42-yr-old 'girl.' I'm sure that neither Rick nor Kent remember that but it was a real turning point

* Sep cell is short for 'Separation Cell,' basically, a time-out room for new arrests.

> Even assuming that Law Enforcement Officers have more experience with force and violence than most people, how much experience is that, really?
>
> I quit counting my Uses of Force at 300. I kept doing the job for ten years after I quit counting, but let's go with 300. Think about that. Is that a lot of experience? Seems like it, but only compared to other people's experience with fighting. Three hundred fights are probably less than five hours of experience.
>
> Fewer than five hours of experience in a subject that may be as complicated as language qualifies me as a leading expert. Go figure.
>
> What does this mean? That officers have seen a lot, compared to most citizens, but they sure haven't seen everything. And that the best experts can give insights, but probably not definitive answers.

for me. It was a huge confidence boost, and I never doubted myself being able to do the job after that. I'm sure I had a smile on my face for a long time too."

Even the rookie doesn't know how she or he will react. If the early encounters go well, like this one, the officer is far more likely to have a long, fulfilling career. Jean retired last year. She was a great partner.

It's not always like that. There are many different ways for an early encounter to go bad, everything from losing your nerve to losing your temper. There are many ways the people around you can respond to the error.

They can be enabling, convincing you it was okay to do whatever you did (enabling a loss of temper predisposes the officer to excessive force later, whereas enabling cowardice creates a Lop).

They can be so mercilessly critical that the rookie becomes afraid to make any decision on his or her own ("sergeant whipped").

They can help the rookie learn and grow into a better way.

Or they can ignore the rookie and hope that he or she can sort it out alone.

There are also many ways that the rookie can respond to the error.

This is one reason why there can never be cookie-cutter responses to how things should work out or how people should be treated. Humans are complex and cops are humans. Further, they are working in complex areas where there isn't often a lot of experience or insight.

That's just rookies. If you can get them to talk, you will often find experienced officers who have had moments of terror or rage. Most controlled it and did the job anyway, but not everyone, not every time.

> Loren Christensen, Vietnam vet, retired police officer, karate champion, and prolific author tells of a time when he got a completely routine radio call—a report of a large drunk in a tavern, assaulting patrons.
>
> Loren reached for the microphone and froze. For reasons that he didn't understand then and still doesn't understand now, he was frozen with fear. He was close to the call. He had handled things like this dozens of times before.
>
> He could not make himself move.

In his career, Loren handled hundreds if not thousands of dangerous incidents. This is the only one where he could not force himself to act. For no apparent reason, other than being human.

And there is the threshold issue—an officer who has handled some very hard things very well may be presented with a situation that overwhelms him, or is outside of his experience far enough that he can't wrap his head around it. Experienced corrections officers who have spent years going hand-to-hand often take excessive risks when asked to perform in an enforcement training scenario. Enforcement officers in a corrections scenario often feel helpless without their weapons.

Sometimes, the situation is very, very bad and you may need to make a decision that you are not prepared to make. Knowing it is legal, right, justified, even *necessary* to take a life does not mean that you can *will* yourself to take a life. Knowing what to do is not the same as doing it.

HARD TRUTH #9

Knowing what to do is not the same as doing it.

I lead seminars for martial artists, teaching what real violence is and how to deal with it. The fine people at *lineofduty.com* gave me permission to show one of their videos at these seminars. The video is from the dashboard camera of Deputy Kyle Dinkheller as he is murdered.

It is chilling in the same way that a masterful suspense movie is chilling. There is no gore in the grainy film . . . but you know what is going on, and feel the reality of it.

> Deputy Dinkheller pulls over a man who is driving erratically. The man gets out of his truck, and begins dancing, chanting, "Shoot my fucking ass." The threat states, "I am a goddamned Vietnam combat veteran, and I am not taking orders from you!" Deputy Dinkheller uses good verbal skills and tries to get the man to calm down. The man closes and is ordered to get back. It sounds like an expandable baton being opened, and the threat is pushed back. It is slightly off-camera, but it is likely that Deputy Dinkheller used the handle of his baton to scrape down the threat's sternum, a pain compliance technique to get him to back off. The threat does back off.
>
> The threat returns to his truck and begins loading a rifle.
>
> Deputy Dinkheller orders him again and again to put the weapon down, to stop loading that rifle, to come back to the patrol car.
>
> The threat is loading a rifle. The threat is obviously in an altered state of consciousness. The threat has stated that he is a combat veteran. Watching the video it is clear that if something doesn't happen he will shoot and kill the deputy.
>
> The deputy cannot break out of his adrenaline loop. The adrenaline loop is when you are so afraid that you just keep doing the same thing over and over without regard to whether it is working.

> Deputy Dinkheeler continues until he is shot. When the threat fires at him, Deputy Dinkheller breaks the adrenaline loop and gets into the fight, but it is too late. A wounded officer with a handgun versus a combat veteran with a rifle.

The situation was a lethal force situation, and Deputy Dinkheller stayed at verbal. The first question is: Why?

Predicting the future (seeing what is going on around you and drawing conclusions about what will happen and what you need to do) is pretty advanced brain stuff. When you are scared, when death is looking you right in the face, the older, primitive part of the brain takes over. Even if your forebrain knows what to do, the hindbrain may be in charge of your body. The hindbrain knows only two things: 1) Death is in the air, and 2) What you are doing right now hasn't killed you yet. And the hindbrain has more than enough power, in most people, to take over completely.

It takes an act of will, sometimes, to do the obvious thing. Your forebrain is not completely shut down. Often, you are thinking very clearly. You just can't move.

> I debriefed one of my junior deputies after he had stood and watched while another deputy was injured. He described it this way, "No, Sarge, I wasn't frozen. I saw everything. I even knew he was going to get hurt. It was like he was in slow motion. Just for whatever reason, I decided not to do anything. It made sense at the time."

In the safety of the classroom, it is so easy to see what must be done, to look into the future, to make the appropriate and justified decision.

Then, there's the second big question: If you get that scared, will you do what you need to do? Or will you keep doing something that is obviously not going to end well?

It's easy to say you will act. Deputy Dinkheller was trained, armed—it's entirely possible that he was tougher than you or me, and smarter than you or me. He didn't act, not until after he was shot (then the hindbrain pretty much knew that the loop was not, in fact, working).

Knowing what to do is not the same as doing it.

And there's the corollary: Sometimes what you know is wrong.

I was searching the property of an inmate who was moving from one housing unit in the jail to another. Pretty routine stuff, something I did several times a night. He had a bunch of what we call "nuisance contraband," things that are against the rules but not weapons. It's not usually worth taking the inmate to Disciplinary Segregation (the "hole") for it. I just threw it away.

The inmate proceeded to get more and more agitated as I threw away more of 'his' stuff. He finally went over the line. It was years ago, but I remember him as frothing at the mouth and swinging his arms. I searched through my mind to find the appropriate "academy approved" technique.

Get this—I'd been a competitive judo player in college, and had studied jujutsu for about four years at that point. Instead of going with what I knew I was good at, I tried to use a technique that I had about one hour of training in, because it was 'approved.'

We wound up rolling around in a wild fight before I thought, "Screw this!" and put him in an arm lock. Damn near broke his arm, too, before he gave up.

Here is a fine line for officers: As long as you go with what you learned at the academy, and from your agency, you can't get in trouble. You can be sued, but if you were within policy, the agency takes the liability. You can't face disciplinary action for following the rules. But you can get your ass kicked, or even be killed by following them blindly.

3.4 What Constitutes a Lethal Threat?

"I had captured an Albanian national while I was in the United States Border Patrol (USBP). I'd had to climb down the bottom of a small cliff to get to the landing. The Albanian had two smugglers who'd waded the river with him. I didn't know it at the time, but, he owed them $2000 US.

I hit the landing and grabbed him. The other two jumped into the water. I made a mistake, and started trying to talk to the Albanian in English and Spanish, essentially interviewing him. The smugglers are yelling at him to jump in with them. I yell at them to have a nice cup of shut-the-fuck-up. What I should have been doing was returning to my vehicle and my partner.

A few seconds later, the smugglers exit the river and come through the brush to my location. I'd say it was all of 12-15 yards from where I was, at the bottom of the small cliff to the river. The brush stopped less than 10 yards from the cliff, so they were effectively 10 yards away from me. They came out armed with rocks, which they began to throw. I was trapped, as my only way out was to scale a small cliff, which would have taken a minute or two, using handholds.* There was no retreat.

Now, when I say rocks I mean rocks the size of baseballs or bigger. As such, they were easy to dodge, but the guys kept closing while they threw them. Also, note they had taken flanking positions, one off each flank, so I had a hard time keeping both in visual (especially when the tunnel vision started). One would throw rocks and threaten while the other moved. I cleared leather and hoped the gun would scare them. I was told, 'Shoot motherfucker. You don't have the guts. Shoot me.' I should have, but didn't. For whatever reason, what was going through my head was the news reports from the next day: 'Border Patrol Agent shoots unarmed man.' Because, see, that's how we look at things like rocks (you can see this when Palestinians throw rocks at Israeli troops). I felt the media would crucify me.

They kept this flanking until one got a hold of my prisoner. I turned and pointed the gun at him and was about to fire. I think

* The officer makes this point because climbing with handholds he could not have defended himself.

he saw it in my eyes and he let him go, turned back and started throwing rocks again.

This went on for about 1,000,000,000,000 years (or around 30 seconds, take your pick), until I was covering one and didn't see the other one throw the rock. I had been ducking and dodging until that time, but this one, I didn't see. I just felt the wind, as it brushed past my shoulder. That really, really scared me. I turned and thought, 'I'm about to die here.' I shot. (My report was very clear—it was not a warning shot. Warning shots are prohibited. I just happened to miss.)

The smuggler I shot at stopped and looked at me. I knew my next shot was going Center of Mass (CoM), and I think he realized this too. He turned and ran and jumped in the Rio Grande, and swam back to Mexico. His partner did too. At this point, my backup was still more than a minute away. The whole thing took less than two minutes.

The smugglers reached Mexico, where the Mexican authorities I'd called, when I first yelled at the smugglers to shut-the-fuck-up, had arrived. The authorities jumped them on the landing, at which point, one of them took off running, and one of them jumped in the river. The one who jumped in the river was shot to death by the Mexican authorities.

Moral—'Death or serious bodily injury' means just that. We're conditioned to think that guns and knives mean lethal force. But there are a number of things that can meet this standard. Also remember that all it takes is something to incapacitate an officer and then someone can stroll up and get the officer's gun and use it against them, like might have happened to me had I been hit with the rock and survived the hit. I would likely not have survived what happened next had they gotten my gun."

There are many lessons in this story—the fact that in isolated circumstances incapacitated cops know they can be easily killed with their own weapons. That things are handled differently, or should be, when back-up is not available. That there is a real fear of how the media will present a use of force incident and that fear sometimes causes officers to take unnecessary risks with their own lives.

That in the United States, an officer cannot shoot a threat for running away, but that in Mexico, they certainly can.

In the "Training" section, we illustrate what may happen and what you should do. Real life is almost infinitely complicated. An officer needs the skills to survive and the judgment (and the freedom) to make decisions. Decisions that will get the job done without getting him, or her, killed.

The agent added:

> "It's so hard to put into words how scared I was. I'd been in a shooting already and had chased down an armed kidnapper in the last year. But I'd never been hunted before, and those smugglers were hunting and stalking me. They were the predators and I the prey. I had to take that away from them and I almost didn't do it. I waited waaaaay too long and hesitated because it didn't seem like lethal force to me even though it very much was. I was also worried about what the public would think about me shooting an 'unarmed' person. The brain thinks what it will in these kinds of incidents, but if you've got your mind straight beforehand about what kinds of situations you'll engage in, then this is less of a problem.
>
> It's terrifying to be hunted so very close in proximity. I wish I could convey what this did to me. It messed me up for a bit, but then I used it. It showed me a hole I didn't know I had. I learned from it."

He summed it up better than I could, especially how a meat-eater learns and gets better.

Once upon a time: Things get chaotic on the streets. Sometimes there are multiple threats. Sometimes it is imperative to get the threat out of the area before the situation degenerates, before friends or family members get involved, for instance. Sometimes the threat, even though handcuffed, still wants to fight. An unfortunate side effect is that, occasionally, the arresting officers don't do a thorough search of the suspect before taking him to jail for booking. I have no idea how many weapons or how much drugs and paraphernalia I have confiscated working booking. Hunting knives, butcher knives . . . I even found a welding hammer once.

> I was searching an arrestee. I had already done a cursory search, just looking for really obvious weapons and had taken the cuffs off before starting the thorough pat search. At the base of his spine, under his shirt, I felt a cylindrical object. I immediately thought, 'knife.' I asked him what it was.
>
> "Let me show you," he said and spun, reaching for it.
>
> I reached to stop his hand and slammed him into the wall, sweeping his legs out from under him, making sure that his head hit the wall, the stainless steel counter, and the floor. He had spun exactly the way I had trained to draw my off-duty gun from under a jacket.
>
> The object was a cigarette lighter. He had hoped to smuggle it into jail since, in a non-smoking facility, a lighter is a very high-value object. A little drunk, he thought that showing it to me quickly would be better in some way than simply answering my question.

Was the force excessive?

Consider—had it been a knife or a gun, had I waited to be sure, there is little guarantee that I would be able to take it away from him without being injured or killed. Even if I had been able to control a hand holding a gun enough not to be shot, there were other people there—officers, civilian staff, and other inmates. There would be no way to keep him from squeezing the trigger.

I'd be lying if I said that this was all a conscious decision. In reaction time tests, I have been able to draw and fire a gun from a level three holster in seven-tenths of a second. Faster, without the 'reaction' aspect. Without the holster, even faster. There was no time for any thought process.

As the situation presented, it was a lethal threat and would have authorized deadly force. The force I actually used was Level 5, damage.

3.5 Feelings, Pain, Damage, and Death

Any use of force can look shocking to a civilian. As a citizen becomes a recruit and then a cadet and rookie and grows into an experienced officer, the bar for 'shocking' will change. Some events are still disturbing—rooms splashed in blood, and broken children stay with you.

One of the concepts inherent in the Force Continuum is that there are different types of bad things that can come from using force and those things have very different values. Death is worse than crippling; crippling is worse than injury; injury is worse than pain; pain is worse than fear.

This seems obvious, but it often feels like there is a big disconnect with civilians, almost as if many civilians don't distinguish between pain and injury or as if many put an equal value between humiliation and death.

> Reaction time: The person who moves first wins, almost always. These are elements of speed and decision making. If you wait, you must first OBSERVE the action. If you don't see it, you will be nailed. Then you ORIENT—the technical term for discerning what the action is. In the example, I OBSERVED the spin and ORIENTED that it was a weapon draw. Then, and only then, can you DECIDE what to do about it. Only after the decision can you ACT. (Some will recognize this as Colonel John Boyd's OODA loop) The person who acts first is three steps ahead. It is almost impossible to go through all four steps fast enough to catch up.
>
> I demonstrate this with ConSim guns. I have two officers with weapons pointed at my chest, and fingers on the triggers. I hold a Sim gun at my side. The officers order me to put the weapon down. Sometimes I comply. If I choose to fire, I consistently get off three shots before the officers can squeeze the triggers. If I side-step, the shots they get off miss.
>
> The cowboy myth of beating someone to the draw . . . is a myth.

> Several years ago I was tasked with taking the underwear from a suicidal, female inmate. The previous shift had 'forgotten' to get all of her clothing.
>
> When an inmate is placed on suicide watch, all clothing is taken and the inmate is issued a paper suit. People have attempted or committed suicide with pants, shirts, shoelaces, belts, and even the elastic from socks and underwear. For policy and liability concerns, we didn't have a choice on this in our agency.
>
> I was uncomfortable—a male sergeant given a direct order to get the underwear from a mentally unstable, suicidal woman. By force, if necessary.
>
> I tried to talk. The kid (adult female, but still a kid) was a mess. Scared of all men, crying, truly suicidal. I broke one of the female officers, Chris, free to try to talk to her. Chris talked for half an hour. It was a pretty heroic effort, but wasn't getting anywhere. It did supply the information I needed.
>
> I snarled at the women, "Ma'am, you're out of time. I'm going to get four officers and we're going to go into your cell and tear your clothes off! I'm tired of waiting! Give them up right now or you are going to have men all over you!"
>
> She gave them up. Chris had been able to get enough information to clue us in that the women had been violently sexually abused in the past. It was only verbal, but I brutally used that history and the fear to get her to comply—all to prevent a use of force.

Here's the deal—I'd rather scare the shit out of someone than hurt them. Rather give them nightmares than take a chance on breaking their bones.

Officers are intimidating—so that they don't have to touch the people they scare into complying.

Wrist locks and pressure points and pepper spray and Taser all hurt, a lot. We use them so that we don't have to use the baton or the fist. Tasers hurt an ungodly amount, but the injury is minimal, no more than the damage from two barbed needles or fish hooks a quarter of an inch deep. Batons and fists work by damage . . . and we use those to prevent using the gun.

When video on the Internet or the local news shows someone screaming at a force incident, look at the injury. If there is no or minor injury, would the other options that might have made for quieter screams resulted in greater injury?

It's not just civilians who fail to understand this. My tactical team was going out on the line for a city riot and one of our senior administration ordered us not to take less-lethal weaponry because they looked 'too intimidating' for the media.

Looking intimidating is part of the point. But by removing the less lethal (some of which looks pretty scary, especially the six-shot 37mm launcher), it also removed our low-level force options. In an attempt to look nicer for the media, the order pushed us significantly closer to using lethal force if things went bad.

3.6 The Nightmare Threat

Not every officer will experience someone like this in his or her career, but all have heard of them

"I was working Holding 2," Sean writes. His duties in that post on that graveyard shift in that jail were to monitor the arrestees held in the cells and prepare to take them to the jail for housing or to the release office if they could be released. One of his first duties was to check the Separation Cells where inmates who had been a problem during the booking process were put in isolation to cool down. Two of the cells were occupied. One held G, who had been in the cell for about three hours. Sean was told that G had "seemed retarded but had been quiet." Sean made the decision, and passed the decision on to his sergeant, that he would move G after an assessment if possible.

The assessment is an art. Sometimes the inmates in Sep Cells are still high or drunk, still angry and dangerous. Usually time calms them down. Some don't calm down. Some had merely taken a dislike to an individual officer and may have no issues at all when a new shift comes on. Some hate all cops. Sometimes how the assessment is done, the demeanor and expectations of the officer, can modify the inmate's behavior and encourage him to behave. Sean went into the cell. He had a conversation with G and told him that if he was quiet he could move to another cell, a more comfortable cell with a mattress, blanket, and phone. G said "Thank you," and Sean went to assess the other inmates on his roster.

Sean returned in about five minutes and walked G down to a cell in another section of the booking area. G asked to use the phone, but refused to enter the cell. Sean tried to coax him in. G just stood there. Sgt. Ron, walking by, noticed something was wrong. The sergeant asked, using a code word, if G had mental problems. Sean said he thought so and asked Ron to stand by.

Both officers tried to talk G into entering the cell. He just stood there, looking first at one, then the other. They decided to take him back to Sep.

Sep cells are uncomfortable. They tend to be cold and boring. No mattress, no blankets, no phone. Just a concrete bench and a stainless-steel toilet/sink combination. G walked back to the sep cell without any serious problem, but he balked again at the door. Both the deputy and the sergeant tried to talk G into entering the cell, but he acted like they weren't there.

Sean put a hand on the back of G's elbow . . . "as soon as I touched him, he attempted to swing around toward me and broke down into a fighting stance . . ." he still didn't say anything. Ron grabbed G's right arm and Sean applied a joint lock to his left arm. G powered through the joint lock.

Sean's a good-sized man, over six-foot and over two-hundred pounds. Ron isn't much smaller. Both were in good shape, experienced fighters and skilled. On top of required training, Sean has studied several martial arts, including karate as a Marine on Okinawa.

Sean knows how to apply a joint lock and he has the size and the strength to back it up. G, a much smaller man, powered out of the hold anyway.

Three men were suddenly struggling in a doorway. The officers made the decision to just push the inmate in and shut the door. They tried. The officers pushed, and the inmate somehow set and twisted. Sean was slammed into the doorframe, and lost his hold on G's arm. Ron went into the cell first and went down.

A third officer, N, heard the commotion, and ran to the cell. Seeing a sergeant down inside the cell, an inmate standing over him and the other, Sean, pushing himself off the wall, N threw a punch that connected with G's face. G sat down on the bench, allowing Sergeant Ron to get to his feet.

The officers tried to make the inmate lie down on the bench. Exiting a cell, through a small door is a high-risk transition—it is tight, limiting mobility. If there are multiple officers, they might trip over each other. An inmate lying down, facing away from the door or kneeling and facing away, usually gives ample time for the officers to exit safely and shut the cell door.

Another officer arrived and wound up under the inmate. Then more officers showed up. Sean delivered a focused blow, a knee strike, to G's lower back. It knocked him forward, but he didn't quit fighting.

More officers arrived. One got a hobble—a special restraint designed to loop a threat's ankles and control his feet—on G. G lifted the deputy into the air, and broke the hobble. That deputy weighed about 260 pounds. The hobble broken was made of one-inch nylon.

Sean writes: "G hadn't said anything during the whole struggle and didn't seem to feel pain at all. In all, six deputies—all but one were much bigger than him and three myself included had lots of training in martial arts and DTs—could barely contain much less control him. Every lock or pain compliance move I attempted he either powered through or ignored. The whole incident from first contact to time of death was just under 1 hour. The struggle itself took 5 or 6 minutes, by far the longest of my career."

Yes. Time of death. When they finally got him handcuffed and his legs controlled, the officers called for the on-duty nurse. That is routine after a Use of Force in this agency. When the nurse arrived, G wasn't breathing. They were unable to revive him. Did the force succeed? Or did his heart fail?

Sean is extremely skilled at applying force. Attitude, experience, size, strength, and training (both martial training and as an officer) come together in him as a nearly perfect package. He would be one of the best bets to handle any unarmed situation. This time a man died, and it was a man they were not trying to kill.

One of the other officers involved said, "Rory, there were six of us and he was a little guy, and I looked around and realized we were losing."

There are two aspects of the nightmare opponent here, two morals to take away from this story. One, simply, is "Here be dragons." In dealing with violent people, scared or angry people, people with emotional, mental, or chemical issues, you will face the extremes of what a human can do. When you hear a story about a mother lifting a car off a baby, remember there is nothing in nature preventing that power, whatever it is, from being misused. That kind of intensity, inhuman strength, imperviousness to pain, and ferocity can also be used to kill.

The second is that unintended consequences are still consequences. Even when you risk your own life to try to restrain someone with minimal harm, they can still die, still suffer an injury. There is no 100% safe technique.

For most people, most officers, death is hard to deal with. It seems to be harder when death is not the intention. When an officer uses deadly force, he or she can understand and explain why it was necessary. When an officer doesn't use deadly force, doesn't feel that deadly force is necessary or justified, and death still happens, it is harder to come to terms with it.

Not all officers will experience a fight like this, where skill, strength, and training might not be enough. Where something that looks easy—'Let's just push him into the cell'—can result in an epic fight and death. Not being there, it is an easy luxury to say that it would be different if it were you, that there must have been a mistake somewhere, that . . .

It's not just stunning to the officers, either. Uninvolved, untrained people follow the same logical thread. Really, how hard could it be to push someone through a doorway? Why can't a big, well-trained officer simply hold a threat until he's tired out?

All that is true, most of the time. It's hard not to use circular logic here, but I'll try. In normal circumstances, a 200-pound man can push a 150-pound man through a door, and do so without serious injury. When a 150-pound man is throwing around four 200-pound men, 'normal' is a moot concept. Extrapolating from normal circumstances (your 150-pound Uncle Bob) will not apply.

Still, it looks wrong to the media, to the populace. One-hundred and fifty pounds of threat versus eight hundred pounds of officers, especially considered with what was written before (more officers means less force), death seems wrong.

Two factors are important here:

One I call the twilight zone or the werewolf factor. Some things don't make sense in a fight. A threat who has never lifted more than a hundred pounds in his life throws a 220-pound officer across a room or jumps over a four-foot fence, ignoring pain, damage, and exhaustion.

The most chilling example was the man who killed Baton Rouge Police Officer Linda Lawrence. In the ensuing hand-to-hand fight, the threat took ten bullets, including a contact wound to the solar plexus and a contact shot to the armpit, described as an armpit-to-armpit 'through and through.'

In the normal world, that is commonly referred to as *dead*, ladies and gentlemen. Instead of sensibly dying, the threat threw officer Lawrence's partner across the room. At the end of the fight, the officer placed his revolver against the threat's forehead and blew a hole in his skull. *The threat got up one more time and tried to engage*. That's why I call it the werewolf factor.

The second factor is when lethal effects result from non-lethal force. If an officer *intended* to stop a threat—not control, contain, or gain compliance, but to end the threat NOW, in other words, when lethal force is necessary—he or she would have gone in with lethal force ready, or applied a lethal tool or technique. When a fatality occurs without the application of a lethal technique, it is solid evidence that death was NOT the officer's goal.

Most fights aren't like this, of course. We call it "Excited Delirium," and there are patterns to it. It often ends badly.

Not all the bad fights are about werewolves. In addition to Excited Delirium and its freakish effects on a use of force, there are also a few mindsets you can't really comprehend until you meet them. Any of these can throw everything you thought you knew out the window. You will be forced to improvise or lose. Often, even a win will end badly, just not as badly as it could have.

> A martial artist I know had a run-in after hours at a bar in an interesting part of town. At the time, he had a little less than twenty years of training in karate. I've met George and he is a superb martial artist, a superb teacher, and I've watched how he handles people. He is clearly a strategist of high order. At the time he had been running the bar, including handling the frequent problem child. So George had lots of training, and it was far from his first fight.
>
> After hours, a group started stealing the bar sign. George ran out and clobbered the biggest. The bad guy went down, blood everywhere. Then, he got up and said, "You want to fight? Let's see what you got."

This was a looking-glass moment. George had trained for besting a martial athlete. He had visualized taking on a knife-wielding psycho. What he got was someone who *enjoyed* fighting.

Think about that. Win or lose, the worst beating you've ever received or handed out is several notches below what he does for *fun.* A trip to the ER for some stitches and a cast, or a night in jail, has all the emotional weight of a hangover—just the price of a little fun.

George got out of there—high-order strategist, remember? But he still thinks about it. The smile on the threat still haunts him.

I present this instance from a civilian point of view instead of an officer's because to some extent this stuff becomes normal for an

Justified, justifiable, prudent, and necessary. In Section 1 you were exposed to the nuts and bolts of the problem. If the threat has Intent, Means, and Opportunity to present a lethal threat, you can respond with deadly force. You can cap his ass. As you are noticing in the "Experience" section, it really doesn't happen that way. If officers shot everyone that they could legally justify shooting, the death count would be ten times what it is.*

In my personal language, 'justified' means it was the right thing to do. 'Justifiable' means it was legal, within policy, and I could convince myself or someone else it was the right thing to do. Catch the subtle difference? Legal and right are not 100% the same. How far apart they are, on any given issue, is a personal judgment. This is where idealists trip up—"justified" force is the goal, the ideal, but not everyone draws that line in the same place. Justifiable becomes the standard where we are required to hold officers accountable.

Justified is the standard I hold, justifiable the legal standard where I am held.

Prudent just means it was a very good idea, that not acting would have been stupid.

Necessary means having no choice—if you had not acted, a truly unacceptable result (say a death) would have resulted.

* "More than one-fourth of the 238 Portland police officers . . . said they pointed guns at people at least once a week. A similar proportion drew once or twice a month. Less than 10 percent said they never drew . . . More than half of the officers in the survey said deadly force was directed against them within the last five years . . . Eighty-six percent said they could have shot someone with full legal justification within the last four years, but chose not to." See "Police Shooting: Who, What and How Many," in the Portland *Oregonian,* April 25, 1992.

officer. I can't speak for everyone, but fighting people who love to fight, love to hurt other people isn't unusual enough to make a blip on my personal radar screen. To a civilian, even one who had trained for twenty years, it was an earth-shaking, mind-bending encounter.

The looking-glass moment. You get to something that you've

prepared for as well and intelligently as you can and it's not what you thought it was. What do you do?

If you take your training as serious business, and you train hard, and play hard—imagine mixing it up with someone who takes your best shot, and laughs because it is sooo much fun. It's been years since he met anybody good enough to hit like that! Yeeeha!

I've been in that mindset, been the one grinning after taking a hit, and it's hard to stop. You see the look in their eyes when they slam you and they see your grin, and they actually start to think that you're not human, not like the people they practice on.

This crosses the line between the nightmare threat and violent subcultures of section 3.8.

There's another mindset too, where it is just a job: "Son, I get paid whether you go to the hospital or not. Make a choice." Martial artists have years of ego built into their training and to fight someone who has no ego about it is chilling and strangely comforting. At the peak, when I was averaging two a week, I spent a lot of time in this mindset. It had a cost, but it was even effective on the manic fight-lovers.

3.7 No More Mr. Nice Guy

About 12:30 A.M. on a Wednesday morning in 1992, Oregon State Trooper Bret Clodfelter pulled over a suspected drunk driver. The driver was going to jail. He was cuffed, searched, and placed in the patrol car. By all accounts, Bret was a nice guy: a good, compassionate man. That was a problem, because there were also two passengers.

It was very late (or very early) and Bret decided to do what a nice guy should do. He offered a ride home to the two men he wasn't going to arrest.

About a half hour later, the Klamath Falls Police Department got a call that there was a State Trooper slumped over the wheel of his patrol car. Trooper Clodfelter had been shot in the back of the head three times. A witness who heard the shooting described two quick shots and a pause before the third shot. The

> third shot had been an execution, what a big game hunter might call 'paying the insurance' to make sure an animal stays dead.

I don't know what to say about this one. The simple fact is that being nice can get you shot. Being an asshole can get you shot, too. Not paying attention can certainly get you shot.

So, what do you tell rookies? We cop out. We say, "Trust your instincts," without ever really explaining what we mean. Did Officer Clodfelter get a tiny twinge of intuition, a subconscious warning that these were the wrong men to transport? Or was the only thing that crossed his mind a fast bit of lead?

Some agencies, many after this incident, wrote policies that no one was to ride in the back of a patrol car unless they were searched and handcuffed. It makes good officer safety sense. Except . . . What officer would say to a traumatized, crying woman, "I'll drive you home, ma'am. But for my safety, I'm required to search and handcuff you?"

This is a dangerous job. It is also a people job. The safest way to do the job is not to do it at all. But someone has to. If not us, then who? This means that sometimes some of us will die. We will die being nice, and we will die doing everything right, and we will die in stupid freak accidents or ambushes.

We all choose to believe that our intuition will give us a little warning and we will listen to it. We believe this as an article of faith because if we ever faced the fact that it might not happen, that any time we come around a corner or enter a building our heads could disappear in a fine pink mist and there is nothing we could do . . . if we faced that fact, we couldn't do the job.

Trust your instincts. It's a cop out, but it is all I have.

3.8 Cultural Differences

One of the biggest changes experience brings is the insight into different cultures. I don't mean minority or immigrant populations. I mean different ways of seeing and understanding the world. Even the most cosmopolitan individual spends time with other people with similar values and beliefs. Officers soon come to understand that the differences in basic thinking between different skin colors and religions are pretty superficial.

The differences between criminals and civilians, on the other hand, can be profound.

This is critical to understand and yet it is very hard for people to accept. We all have assumptions about some very basic things. Because everyone in our experience has expressed similar feelings, we believe that they are more-or-less universal human values.

Here is an example: the importance of children. If you are an average citizen and a parent, your children are an important part of your life, if not the most important. This is a GOOD value. This is as it should be.

In the subculture that officers deal with, they can point at mothers who have prostituted their children for enough drugs to get through the day. Killed their children, so that they would not complicate a possible romantic relationship with a drug source. Men who have fathered more than thirty children and are completely unconcerned with providing for them—"That's what welfare is *for*," one told me with obvious contempt at my ignorance.

This is a decades-old story from a newspaper in my (at the time) hometown. A woman was charged with child neglect, abuse, and reckless endangerment. Neighbors had complained because of the smell coming from her apartment. When police responded they found a baby in a filthy diaper crawling on the floor. Bowls of milk and plates of peanut butter sandwiches had been left out on the floor. The woman was afraid that her new boyfriend might dump her if he knew she had a child, so she would leave the baby, sometimes for days at a time.

She was outraged at the charges and was quoted in the paper insisting that she loved her baby and that anyone who saw them together would know that.

As a corrections officer, I was able to directly see things that Enforcement officers often miss. Inmates, over time, would become bored, or relax their suspicion of the uniform, and they would talk to me. On many occasions, they simply became comfortable and I could listen to their conversations because they had forgotten an officer was there. I have read the journals of child molesters and searched through the sketches of serial killers.

I am privileged to know two men, both war heroes, both of whom have had to kill a man with a knife in war. It still haunts them almost forty years later, haunts them in the frequent nightmares and flashbacks and doubts about their basic humanity. These are good men who did the necessary thing, and they are paying a terrible price for it. They are paying that price because they are normal, good men.

How different is the basic wiring of a human, arrested for stabbing another human who can say, "It was the most awesome feeling in the world. Ever since that day I've been looking for a chance to do it again without getting caught." His eyes are shining as he says it. For him, taking a life was an act that made him a god.

The enforcement officers, except for investigators, will rarely have these conversations, rarely hear how the threat sees his world. But they will see the results. Not just in the broken bodies, but in the way the threat sometimes responds when caught. Sometimes, an inability to see that anything was wrong.

> I remember a child molester completely bewildered. He didn't see that there was anything wrong with what he had done. It was his daughter, right? Why was that any different than his shoes? He could do what he wanted with his shoes, right? That was what 'his' means, right? Well, it was his daughter . . . . He honestly didn't see the distinction.

I'm trying not to get too clinical or technical here. These are things that officers have to work out on their own through experience, through trial and error. When I went through the Academy, I don't recall the words Narcissistic Personality Disorder (NPD), or Antisocial Personality Disorder (APD) coming up.

Sometimes, outside of class, I'm not sure the labels are that useful. They give the impression that this attitude is like disease, something that can be cured, not really anyone's fault. The things we call 'personality disorders' are ways of seeing the world and habits of behavior.

The personality disorders are not something someone *has;* they are labels for who the person *is*.

They are very different, but get to the same place: the NPD thinks that he is so special, so great, that he is entitled to whatever he desires. The APD thinks that others are so inconsequential that they have no say in anything the threat decides—that they have no rights that outweigh the threat's desires. From opposite directions they come to a similar place: other humans exist to be used.

Many of the threats that officers deal with, almost all, will have this worldview. It is a subculture and it is self-reinforcing. Imagine a world without shame or guilt (because whatever the criminal wants is a right). A marginal world where might does in fact make right. Where information is a tool and a weapon and disinformation is habit.

Rookies come to this world fresh, assuming that the rules of society they know apply here—it's the same country, right? The same city the rookie was raised in, sometimes. And all people are pretty much the same, right?

In the civilized world, people need a reason to lie. If there is no discernible motive for lying, it's a reasonably safe bet that a citizen is telling the truth. One of the most painful lessons that rookies have to learn, and something that has fooled politicians, reporters, and well-meaning people, is that in the criminal world, for criminals, there must be a reason to tell the truth. The default value is to lie.

"Sergeant Miller," she was a new nurse in the jail, a nice person with a big heart, "Would I get in trouble if I took an inmate home?"

"Yes."

"I don't mean escape or anything. She's a good girl, and she's never been in trouble before. She doesn't have a place to stay when she gets out. She's really only here for a big misunderstanding."

"Did she tell you that? Have you checked?"

"Well, yes, she did but she doesn't have any reason to lie. She doesn't know I'm thinking about offering her a place to stay. Just until she gets on her feet."

"Let's take a look."

The 'good girl' who had 'never been in trouble before' had almost ten years of criminal history—drugs, prostitution, identity theft, and stealing. She'd found a kind nurse and spun a story. The nurse was smart enough to ask a few questions. Otherwise, she might have let this person into her home and with this person would come her drug and prostitution contacts, and they would have a kind person who would be easy to influence and eventually to intimidate and blackmail. A jail nurse, after all, has access to both drugs and inmates.

". . . doesn't have any reason to lie" deserves a deeper look, also. The world that criminals live in is dangerous, and there is very little you can count on. Information is a source of power, and information given away can be a source of vulnerability. In this environment, lying is the default value. It is nothing so mundane as a habit; it is just a good survival skill. Normal people need a reason to lie. Members of the criminal subculture need a reason to tell the truth.

There are other, minor subcultures, too.

> The arresting officers brought in a guy and warned us he was a fighter. He was old (or so it seemed to me, mid-fifties, which seem less old now, as I move toward fifty). He had been pepper-sprayed and had a gash above his eye, either from falling or a baton.
>
> The old guy struggled and squirmed as we brought him in, searched him, and took the cuffs off. We calmed him down, used very soothing voices, and got him to a chair so that a nurse could look at his laceration. When the wound was cleaned and steri-stripped, he relaxed, took a deep breath and said, "You all have been real nice to me, so I'm sorry. It's time to make you boys fuck me up." He tried to swing. I was a relative rookie, but I'd been working the counter enough that I had quite a few fights by then. My partner was even more experienced, so we were able to pull him to the ground and cuff him before he could do any damage. We carried him to a cell, took off the cuffs, and left him alone to cool off.
>
> I came back an hour or so later. "Hey," I said, "You were

doing real good. There was no reason to fight. You'd probably get released in an hour or so if you hadn't fought."

He looked like a small, sad old man. "I know. But I was in jail. If I didn't fight when I came to jail I wouldn't be a man."

That was it. In his world, his culture, he had to fight. He had no illusion about winning, but he couldn't live with himself if he did what we considered the sensible thing.

How does this all apply to force? Profoundly. Possibly more importantly, it is a missing element of how officers and citizens see force.

Just as the courts use a "reasonable person" standard, we have a similar assumption about people. We believe that force is dangerous, hurts, and is wrong. Normal, sane, people don't like danger or pain. The problem is that these aren't facts, but social assumptions. That is the reason for the examples on child neglect. Caring for your children is one of the greatest biological imperatives, yet in the subcultures of crime (and particularly addiction), children are not always valued as highly as normal, healthy people think they should be valued.

Mediation and compromise work because two people are willing to put in the effort to avoid the alternative. They are predicated on people disliking the pain and danger that could result if negotiations fail. That works for almost everybody.

There are a few individuals, however, who enjoy violence. They are confident enough in their skill that they don't consider it scary or dangerous to them; or they are confident enough in other people's meekness to arrive at the same decision.

These are the ones that officers sometimes fight. With this group, all of our assumptions and plans about how to avoid force, and what level of force should be required, can be invalid.

You must also remember one of the fundamental truths about violence: Violence works. It is something that bad guys use to get what they want. When people look for the sources of violence or seek peace, this is the elephant in the room that everyone ignores. As long as violence works, some people will use it.

3.9 Altered States of Mind

Most people will never commit a serious violent crime. For all but a few, violence is not the way problems are solved. Even for those few who were raised and are comfortable with using violence as a tool or form of communication, they avoid fighting with officers. Unless you are both sure that you will win *and* sure that you will not be identified, fighting with officers is not a high percentage option.

So, obviously, most people who do choose to fight with officers are not in a normal frame of mind. Some are extremely emotional, some are drunk or on drugs, some have mental illnesses. Each of these categories can be broken down. We can talk about them ad infinitum and explore the nuances, but in a crisis moment, the differences don't matter as much as you think.

An intensely depressed person may create a situation called "suicide by cop," where they threaten first themselves, and then someone else—often the officer—with a handgun, leaving the officer no choice but to fire.

A very enraged person, regardless of reason, may just lash out, trying to hurt anything and everything he can.

A terrified person may lash out also, perceiving a routine handcuffing as a survival threat, and fight like a panicked animal.

Different drugs, from alcohol to PCP, affect different people in different ways. From hallucinations to a feeling of confidence so intense that it seems perfectly possible to fight a bunch of officers to drugs that seem to almost erase the human aspects of the mind. The only thing they have in common is that I have yet to see a drug that makes the user smarter. *Think* he's smarter, yeah. But actually smarter? No.

Mental illness is another big category. Manic episodes can bring on confidence that inspire risky or even suicidal behavior, and depression can lead to suicide or destroying the valuable things in life. Schizophrenia can place the sufferer in a world different from what the rest of us share, and autism disorders can leave the individual unable to understand concepts like 'giving-up.'

This is one of the areas where the real world, the natural world, refuse to fit into a box that civilized people, people who believe in justice, would like. More than any other area, these are the uses of force that outrage citizens.

Here are the facts:

1) About citizens and what we want to believe: It's written into our laws, and maybe our genetics, that *motive matters*. We distinguish between accidental manslaughter and premeditated murder. The taking of life in self-defense is justifiable. The taking of the same life out of boredom is callous indifference. So we want to believe, maybe need to believe, that the man charging his children with a knife because he feels that he can do what he wants with his children (and they broke a lamp) should be treated differently than the same man doing the same thing because his medicines failed and he can't resist the voices any more.

That's what we want.

2) Force stops violence. The man slicing a woman's face with a razor may be an Emotional Disturbed Person (EDP) whose medicines failed, but he will not be stopped by a kind word. In the time that you could formulate the thought and get the words out, the victim will be filleted, choking on her own blood.

The collision of these two facts is what outrages people. Force will be used, will have to be used, on EDPs, unless our society changes to the extent that we no longer protect the innocent.

Emotionally Disturbed, mentally ill or just suffering from a bad drug reaction, they don't deserve force, not in the sense of justice, not as some kind of punishment for their choices because the behaviors may not be choices. But society needs to protect the victims, and often the EDP as well.

However, it is even worse than that. As you remember from section one, the threat chooses if force is to be used. At any point, merely by stopping bad actions and letting himself or herself be handcuffed, the threat can prevent force from being used. The threat also decides when he will give up. That is what ends the force.

Both of these are rational choices. Decisions. The nature of an altered state of consciousness is that the decisions made may not be rational.

If the threat is not responding to words, then verbal skills are off the table. Even if there was time to talk, which there often isn't. If the threat is not responding normally to pain (sometimes not feeling it, but sometimes not responding to the bargain inherent in pain compliance), then a low-level technique may be off the table as well. The threat may not even respond to exhaustion in a normal way (see sidebar: Swarming). No other option but damage may be available.

This is hard to accept—with any sense of justice, someone who is not in control of his behavior deserves less force than someone who is choosing to be a threat. He certainly doesn't 'deserve' more and it is unfair that he is more likely to die, not less, because of a rare inability to surrender.

It's NOT fair, but force is NOT ABOUT FAIR. It is about getting the job done and keeping people safe with the least injury that you can. It is horrible that a kid with a mental illness, and all of those cards stacked against him, is also at greater risk to die at the hands of the men and women sworn to protect him. It is NOT fair, but life isn't fair and in this case it is nature, life itself, dispensing the injustice, not the officer.

I am going to present two cases here, partially to show the problems of force issues with EDPs, but also to examine the perception gap. I will use only the newspaper source.

These are hard for me to write about. The information is public, so I could list names, dates, and places, directly quoting the people who said things when they were hurting. I'm not sure there is value in that.

Once upon a time, a young man took about thirty times the normal dose of hallucinogenic mushrooms. A 29-year-old single mother woke up to find the young man in her apartment, standing over her. He was wearing a t-shirt and shorts. His feet were bare.

The mother ordered him to leave. He started to, then threw a pillow at her, and "rubbed her pants" (and here I wonder about

> Swarming—when enough officers are present there is a technique called swarming, where the officers try to grab limbs and body, and through weight and strength, bear down and tire out the threat. (We do, in fact, sometimes refer to it as a 'pig pile.') By avoiding impact, joint locks, and pressure points, it is a relatively low-risk-of-injury technique. Sometimes. The officers in a swarm are vulnerable to having their weapons taken away and used against them. We all have a story about officers getting control and having two different officers claim to have the threat's right leg, only to find out that one has been wrestling with a fellow officer. I've been hit by swinging restraints in a swarm.
>
> There is another danger in the swarm. The technique depends on the threat getting tired. A small percentage of people in altered states of consciousness—see "Nightmares," section 3.6—don't quit when they get tired. Whether through extreme fear, or drugs, or mental illness, they continue to fight sometimes until their heart fails or they are literally suffocated. Since they were in a fight up until the last moments, the officers are unaware that the threat is crashing until he suddenly goes limp.

the reporter—was the woman wearing the pants? If not, why mention it? If so, was there a deliberate attempt to make this sound like goofy, stoned action, rather than the prelude to a sex crime?). He lay down on the rug, and she called the police.

The article says that she reported that the threat was on mushrooms, and dispatch did not report that to the responding officers. That strikes me as something of a non-issue in that officers would need to deal with his behavior. The behavior was clearly bizarre, but whether it came from drugs, or a schizophrenic episode, or something else has little bearing on getting the man restrained. The paramedics would need that information.

The woman then ran to her daughter's room. The threat followed her and forced the door open. The woman and her daughter fought with the man. They seemed to be winning when the first officer arrived. The woman (and, I assume, her daughter)

> fled. The officer tried to talk to the threat. The threat alternated between sitting quietly and lunging at the officer and said some relatively bizarre things.
>
> The article says that the officer backed out of the apartment and the threat followed, at one point leaping a fence. The threat ran away, and then ran back, pulling down his shorts.
>
> When back-up officers arrived, they used beanbag rounds (a 'less lethal' round, cloth bags filled with birdshot and fired from a shotgun, claimed to be the equivalent of being hit by a baseball thrown by a major league pitcher) and the Taser. The threat did not go down and the officer is quoted that "the threat remained standing in the midst of a Taser cycle."
>
> The threat then tried to get into a patrol car where there was a rifle locked into the console. One of the officers fired three rounds into the threat's body. He continued to try to get into the car. The officer fired a fourth round into the threat's head. This one was fatal.
>
> By the time it was over, there were three officers there, each of them considerably larger than the threat. The article concludes by quoting the family's attorney, calling the incident a ". . . totally avoidable tragedy." They dealt with a "confused" suspect by shouting commands and firing weapons. "They should have called an ambulance, not the cops."

Did he mean the terrified woman, who had been groped, should have put the welfare of the home invader above that of her daughter? She was, after all, the one who called the cops. Interesting.

When I read stuff like this, I try not to be judgmental, but it is usually easier not to read it. Everyone involved—the family of the victim, the reporter, maybe even the attorney (though his professional ethics would require him to be just as adamant for the opposite cause if he were paid by the other side)—are trying to do the right thing. The family is hurt and wants closure and maybe vengeance. The reporter sees badges and guns and numbers and the weight of authority on one side—and on the other side, a poor guy who messed up his head and died. He wants justice as he sees it.

Still. The officer did try talking. He was lunged at. He retreated and he was followed. When cover arrived, they attempted Tasers (pain compliance) and beanbag rounds (impact/damage tools). It is not, and never has been, required to hit every level of the force continuum before advancing to the next, but it appears that these officers did.

Did they have a duty to act? Unless you can argue that when a strangely behaving man breaks into your home the officers don't need to respond for fear of disturbing the invader; they absolutely had a duty to act.

If the man had quit, if he had even run away, this could have ended very differently. But when he did run away, he came back.

There are two real questions to consider:

1) Did the threat have the Intent, Means, and Opportunity to present a lethal threat to the officers or others? Intent is the hardest to show, especially in cases of altered mental states. The threat had already done a home invasion crime. Historically, these often become some of the most brutal crimes—torture murders, helter-skelter stuff. Mushrooms certainly did not make these either less likely or more predictable. If you are thinking of friends you have seen stoned, who were harmless, I have to ask if they ever broke into a home, "rubbed" a woman's "pants" and then forced open a door to get access to an eight-year-old girl.

Even then, the officers did not use lethal force. They did not use lethal force until the threat tried to get into the patrol car. The weapon in the front seat of the patrol car is usually either a twelve-gauge shotgun, or an M4 rifle with a 20- or 30-round magazine. I do not know what this agency supplies, but the article says "rifle," so I will guess the M4.

Had the officers intended to use lethal force, they would have brought the rifle with them. Again, I don't know the configuration of these patrol cars. The article says that the weapon was locked, but the models that I have seen, have concealed quick release buttons in (to my mind) obvious places.

Intent—probable, especially if the threat was fighting to get to the rifle. Means? That was what he was fighting to get. Opportunity? If he got the rifle, he could have sent as many as thirty rounds into the neighborhood—everyone within 400 meters, even those behind walls, would have been in danger.

2) The second question is whether three big officers could and should have attempted to wrestle with the threat. Wrestling is the same level of force as pain compliance, a level that had already failed.

Ignoring a Taser is not something to take lightly. In my agency, officers who carry Tasers are required to experience being hit with them. The pain is so intense that it literally wiped out my brain for several seconds. When you have seen men that you know to be very tough, dedicated and experienced fighters fall to the ground screaming—it sets an expectation in your head. When you then see someone ignore it, it is a little awe-inspiring. More than a little.

In order to beat someone hand-to-hand who will not give up or respond to pain, you either need to shut down his brainstem (as the final bullet did) or break bones until he cannot move. The officers' choice would be to go into that situation, recognizing that in close proximity, the threat could access weapons from their belts, and knowing that they might not win, or that they may have to cripple or kill the threat in any case. Should they risk it?

Maybe. This is what the jury will decide in the eventual lawsuit. Some would, some wouldn't. Some might have tried and succeeded. Some might have tried and failed.

There is one technique that probably would have worked. In judo, it is called *hadaka jime*. The military teaches it as the sleeper hold. Sometimes, but very rarely, people die when this technique is applied. No technique is 100% safe, anymore than any technique is 100% effective. Many agencies, after some highly publicized deaths in the 1980s, have forbidden the sleeper hold. The outcry over that technique—and again, everyone involved was trying to do the right thing—removed the one tool most likely to have prevented this death.

This was a tragedy, and there are far too many variables to say, for sure, that it could have been handled in a better way.

One more case:

> The call came in after midnight on a cold December night. A barefoot, shirtless man was crossing one of the many bridges in Portland, Oregon, walking down the centerline and swinging something variously described as a stick or a club. The responding officer drove alongside the man and tried to talk to him. He was ignored. He drove a little farther to get some safe distance and got out of the car, with his Taser ready.
>
> Tasers have a laser sight. The red dot of a laser on your chest is a pretty clear signal. Few ignore it. In this case, the threat advanced on the officer, swinging his stick. When a 260-pound man with a club charges you, what are your options?
>
> The officer Tased him. The man went down. Then he got back up, and came at the officer again. By the time it was over, the threat had received four Taser shocks and six strikes with a baton. No death. No serious injury.

Did the officer have a duty to act? Absolutely. With a threat in a clearly altered state of consciousness (do I need to point out the clues to that?), walking at night on a dark road swinging a club, the potential dangers to both the threat and the public were real and immediate. What level of resistance did the threat show? A 260-pound man with a club could easily be a lethal threat. Clearly the threat showed Means (size and weapon); Intent (advancing swinging his weapon even when faced by a weapon); and Opportunity (advancing into range). The officer could easily have justified deadly force. He did not use deadly force.

The newspaper and some advocacy groups were outraged. There were two facts the officer did not know at the time, and *could not have known.*

The first is that the threat was only fifteen years old. At 260 pounds and with a weapon would that have been relevant even if the officer knew it?

The second was that the altered state of consciousness was due to autism.

First, the officer was there to deal with a behavior, not a diagnosis. Second, despite movies that present autism as a benign and harmless disorder it does not make people harmless. My children are both high-functioning autistics. Through them we know many other autistic children and adults, some of them quite severe. My children did not naturally understand the difference between petting a kitten and strangling one, or why eyes, which look so much like marbles, can't be pulled out to play with. We know more severely affected children who cannot be schooled with other children because they pose a danger to them.

Autistic people absolutely need compassion, but they also need to be prevented from hurting others or themselves. Sometimes, officers will be the ones called on to prevent that. If the autistic threat (or schizophrenic or drunk or drugged or . . . any altered state) uses violence or starts to use violence, the officer must use force to stop the violence. The best counselor in the world will not get a handle on the situation with words when the patient is charging, swinging a club. The counselor will run, something the officer, with the duty to act, cannot do.

There is one other, very relevant detail that affects how I see this event.

A large man, approaching, swinging a club and ignoring a weapon or orders to stop clearly justifies deadly force. The officer chose to use a Taser. The Taser is a single-shot weapon. If one of the probes misses, or if one of the wires break, or if the threat is one of those rare individuals unaffected by the electrical discharge, the officer must remove the dart cartridge and replace it with another. That is a fine motor skill and takes time. The Taser the officer used had a maximum range of 21 feet. Ergo, when this threat was tased, he must have been within 21 feet of the officer.

That is an interesting number. In an experiment called the Tueller drill,* trainers have shown, time and again, that an individual with

* Dennis Tueller, "How Close is too Close?" *SWAT Magazine,* March 1983.

a knife can close 21 feet, consistently, before an officer can draw his handgun.

Had the Taser failed completely, the officer involved never would have had time to draw another weapon before the threat was on him. Not only did he use a lower force than was authorized, he literally gambled his life that it would work. He *risked his life* to use a lower level of force than was authorized to stop a man attacking him—and the media was outraged.

HARD TRUTH #10

Surrendering is a learned skill.

There is so much in Hard Truth #10; it leads to so many things that seem unfair. A true professional criminal knows the game. He knows when he is caught and how far he can push and still be taken into custody without injury.

Arrest, jail, even prison are just the cost of doing business, and for some, they are necessary stops in the lifestyle. A low-level street hustler often relies on occasional trips to jail to get healthy and take a break from the weather and constant tension. Bad guys are least likely to get injured during an arrest because they know when and how to quit.

First-time offenders, people who are regular citizens but have made a mistake or temporarily lost control, know that they should surrender but don't know how. Where a criminal might try to show defiance safely, with verbal insults and threats and take care not to present a physical threat, a clueless kid may assert his independence by refusing to show his hands—which not only shows defiance, but also implies a weapon and justifiably draws a greater level of force.

Saddest of all are the emotionally disturbed, the mentally ill, and some under the influence of drugs. They may not be able to hear or understand the officer, may not recognize the message in a drawn weapon, and may not be able to think to surrender, much less know how to do so safely. The fact that they have no choice, that none of this is evil, or badness, or blameworthy doesn't change the fact that

> From the other side, in the excellent book, *Code of the Streets,* Elijah Anderson points out that people who live in high-crime neighborhoods are rarely injured in street crime incidents because they know how to get mugged. Not only when arrested, but even when being mugged, surrendering is a learned skill.

officers may still have to step in and stop them. And the threat, not the officer, determines how much it will take.

3.10 The Threshold

> The paramedic said, "I had a partner once, great guy. One of the best. Fun to work with really, really good on a hot call. One day we had an MVA (motor vehicle accident) with multiple casualties. It was bad. We triaged and I was stabilizing one of the casualties and I looked over and my partner was trying to put the head back on the baby.
>
> He'd put the head on and it would roll off and he'd put it back on and it would roll off. He just kept doing it over and over. He was never the same after that."

These are third-hand stories because the people who have experienced them almost never talk about them. You hear it from partners or you see it yourself.

Emergency Services (EMS) personnel (fire, police, paramedics) exist to deal with things the rest of society would rather not. Sometimes it is simple math: evacuating a burning building is dangerous enough and rare enough that it doesn't make economic sense to train everyone to do it.

Sometimes, it is common sense: dealing with dangerous things well requires equipment, training, and a certain psychology. It is safest to have professionals handle dangerous things whenever possible.

And sometimes it is deep emotion. There are things out there that are not psychologically healthy to experience. Crime scenes. Victimized children. Crushed pedestrians. Burned former people. Rape victims. It makes sense to limit the number of people who experience these things as much as possible. It, hopefully, preserves everyone else's emotional health.

Being strong enough to see this stuff isn't always enough. Sometimes, especially if you go into investigations, Crisis Negotiations, or Hostage Rescue, you need to not only withstand the sights sounds and smells but also to actively work and function in that arena.

Most officers will have emotional fallout when they respond to a heinous crime. They will see and hear the victim, get the initial statements, offer what comfort they can . . .

Then the investigator will come in, and she will ask deeper questions. No matter how compassionate or skilled the detective, she will be helping the victim remember some very dark things, and the detective will hear it all.

(Don't misunderstand me. I'm not looking for sympathy for the officers here. The sympathy goes to the victim. I'm trying to explain something else, but it takes some foundation.)

The investigator will also interview the perpetrator. If the interview (and, later, the interrogation) goes well, the investigator will spend a lot of time in the head of someone who enjoys things a normal person isn't capable of. She will read the suspects' journals. Some of the best can make friends with child molesters again and again in order to get the suspects to talk.

Most people, most officers, would have a hard time with that. Most people, officers, and even paramedics have trouble with decapitated children.

Here's the deal: some people hit their threshold. When you run into that thing, the event that is too ugly or too close to home, you're done.

We don't know where our thresholds are. Not until we hit that wall. Will it be our first shooting? The death of a partner? Suicide of a co-worker? An arson murder? The child victim who looks so much like our daughter?

Most emergency services personnel will never find the limit. Sometimes it will be a relatively quiet career. Sometimes they will go twenty or more years and never find the thing that pushes their buttons or the bad thing they never imagined. Some compartmentalize extremely well. Some maintain psychological health with strong families and outside interests.

But we know the threshold is out there.

That's why we rarely mock this type of burn-out. The most insecure officers might, hiding behind bravado, talking about weakness in others to keep from wondering about their own. I think most of us are too aware for that.

3.11 It's an Integrated World

We're all profilers. You're a profiler, too. Think about it. You see a big, shiny, clean pickup in a big city and you automatically think masculinity issues. The ability to read people in the context of their environment is something that all humans do. Salesmen are excellent at it. So are bartenders.

Humans are both genetically prepared and socially conditioned to integrate huge amounts of information. Babies have been tested and shown a sense of rhythm or number—if five rubber duckies disappear behind a screen and only four pop out, even a baby knows that something is up.* It is part of who we are as humans—we see patterns and draw conclusions in ways that no computer, as yet, can do.

I mentioned at the end of 'training' that an ugly use of force is a big, complex, fast thing, and that the decisions will be made subconsciously and on partial information. People of good heart will make compassionate decisions. People with a will to live will make survival decisions. People with both will make *good* decisions.

I deliberately brought up profiling in the first line of this section to push buttons. We all profile, all the time—profiling is merely using what you see combined with experience to draw conclusions. It is accurate whenever it isn't. I assume—or profile—that all big, four-wheel-drive farm trucks are manual transmissions. I'm always a little

* Izard V, Dehaene-Lambertz G, Dehaene S (2008) Distinct Cerebral Pathways for Object Identity and Number in Human Infants. PLoS Biol 6(2): e11. doi:10.1371/journal.pbio.0060011

thrown off to get in one and find it's an automatic. I expect Siamese cats to be slightly high-strung and louder than other cats. I expect German Shepherds to be extremely protective of their human family.

All of these things are true often enough that you can bet on them, but all of them have exceptions.

As my wife says, people want to believe that they are their own special little snowflake. Everyone *is* slightly unique. Simultaneously, everyone is largely the same—people need to eat, almost all have a need to be part of a group. They prefer pleasure to pain, though some define those two things differently than most of us . . . humans generally have enough in common that they can communicate. People have far more commonalities than they do differences.

There is a marginal area, too, a collection of common differences. If one type of vehicle has certain features in common—easy to buy used, for cash; relatively cheap; known to have many places to hide contraband—that car will be on local cops' minds as likely delivery vehicles for low-level drug dealers. If local gangs wear something specific, wearing that thing is a good indicator that the person is (or wants to be) a gang member.

But sometimes, it is just a clueless high school kid who watches too many videos. *Profiling is accurate whenever it isn't.*

Racial profiling is one of those things that isn't as common as the heat it gets. Race is a factor—not because there are inherent differences in humans of different colors or beliefs, but because criminal networks run through ties of friendship and blood. In my area, crack is run by black gangs and meth by white gangs; most of the traffickers in heroin are Hispanic, and the designer drugs are sold by college kids—overwhelmingly white, but not exclusively.

So a fairly expensively modified but old muscle car, driven by two white guys with shaved heads in a black neighborhood won't get pulled over, but will be watched. With no customer base in the area, the odds are poor that any drugs will be found.

If your ears twitched and you thought, "What about guns, you racist cop?" Congratulations, that's some good profiling. But in most jurisdictions, just having guns in a car isn't a crime. Hence the watch, but not the pull over. Again, GOOD INSTINCTS.

See the same car in a meth-dealing area, yeah, you wait for an excuse to pull them over.

This is all changeable by time and place. I personally feel that races are something of a myth, a belief that we cling to in order to feel special. As the world changes, as television brings more common ground socially, and as different groups travel, meet, develop relationships, and have children; I think the concept of race will fade.

Not yet. For now, it is one factor among many: Sometimes a major factor, sometimes a detail.

Thinking of profiling only in terms of racial profiling can be a distraction from the crux. The crux is this: There is a lot of information available in any given situation. How much is seen, how accurately it is perceived, and how conclusions are drawn is a matter of skill and experience. Often, a matter of previous knowledge.

There are certain cultures in which a knife is almost always carried and is the preferred weapon. This is a factor when an officer approaches a threat who is, or may be, of that culture. Common sense says that if there might be a knife involved, you advance with a gun drawn. Knives are very fast, ugly weapons at close range, much faster to deploy than a handgun.

Simple cultural awareness from experience—*that group often uses knives*—in the eyes of naïve, but well-meaning people is presented as racial profiling. "The officer had a gun drawn because the suspect was (name your ethnicity or religion.)"* In most instances, cultural awareness is considered a good thing and rewarded; in this instance, it can be denigrated.

This sets up an ugly dynamic. "Special knowledge" is one of the recognized influential circumstances that can alter the appropriate level of force. This is true despite policy or law. Saying it is illegal or improper to consider cultural differences does not magically make those differences unimportant. It forces the officer to either risk his or her life for the sake of political correctness, or it forces the officer to make survival decisions and then lie about the reasons behind those decisions.

* I am aware of two religions that *require* their members to carry a blade.

In a fast use of force, lots of the decision-making is subconscious. This makes it hard to study. A laboratory can never recreate the fear of a real situation, or make the officer believe that if he fails, he will really die. Surveys are subjective, and often what the person remembers is what they want to remember or people answer questions not with the truth, but with what they believe the truth should be.

This brings up questions that I cannot answer here. I will tell you what I believe, at the end.

What about profiling purely on appearance, straight-up racial profiling? How much does recognition of 'other.' independent from 'special knowledge,' influence decision-making?

People are tribal, and people cut more slack within family than within tribe, and within tribe than within nation, and within nation than within species, and . . . An average officer is less likely to give his mother a traffic ticket than your mother; more likely to give another officer the benefit of doubt than a lawyer; more likely to contribute to Red Cross relief efforts for a disaster in New Orleans than in Indonesia. This is pretty universal.

Honestly, I see it less in officers than in average citizens. Here's the deal. Because I was raised in cowboy country that was predominately white, almost every non-white person I know, I know from the job. And knowing someone from the job is far from a random sample.

Almost every (black/Hispanic/gay/name-your-group) person I know is either a hero or a criminal. Almost all of the heroes would say that they are just ordinary, average guys, but that's horseshit. They're heroes. Simple fact is that the heroes are heroes and there isn't any variation in color. White heroes are not any better or worse than black ones. Nor is any color of a criminal more depraved than any other color of criminal.

More than any other group in the United States, officers and soldiers trust other officers and soldiers to watch their backs and keep them alive. You only have to do that a couple of times (or call for back-up when you really need it) before you are aware that you don't give a damn about what color, or gender, or religion, or sexual orientation shows up. You care that they are competent, that they have the heart to fight if it is necessary, and they have the judgment to make the right decision. Everything else is irrelevant.

Steven Barnes, a very good friend (and hero) makes the case that at a subconscious level, we 'other' people who do not look like us. It may be just cutting someone 5% less slack or extending 3% less trust.

We don't have the science right now, to know how much or in what circumstances, or even if it is a negative to 'other' people who do not look like us. If 3% less trust balances a 3% more likely to be violent for the same 'othering,' it may not be a negative, but prudent.

Your brain sees many things, correlates them, and draws conclusions in the blink of an eye. Years ago, an officer killed someone that I knew. Details were sketchy, but the officer fired when the threat first refused to show his hands and then reached under his jacket. For his ID? For a weapon that he didn't have?

The officer was crucified in the media and it was presented as a racial incident. I always wondered . . .

The officer didn't know the threat, but I did. He was extremely violent, extremely dangerous, and very manipulative. The officer had no way to know that.

I often wondered if, subconsciously, the officer had recognized a disfigurement on the threat's face as an old gunshot wound. The threat had been shot, previously, in a robbery or drug deal gone bad (I don't remember the story the threat told me—or stories—and didn't write them down, not thinking it would matter later when I started writing).

Was one of the contributing factors to that shooting a subconscious recognition that the threat was no stranger to gun violence? I'll never know.

3.12 Abuse of Power and Excessive Force

This book is about force issues, and applying force is one of the most basic forms of power. The weapons an officer is given, the training, the badge, and all that the badge symbolizes make for a potent expression of power. This power clearly could be twisted. Citizens are

Something to think about:

Crack and flake cocaine are chemically the same. The penalties for possession and distribution, in many jurisdictions, are wildly different. Is it because crack is used more often by poor, black folk in the U.S., and flake tends to be used by richer, white people? Is it racism?

Or is it because for every death associated with the flake cocaine trade (often a user, richer and whiter) there are at least twenty in the crack trade (almost always poor and black)? Would it also be racism to treat the drugs as the same and do nothing to prevent these killings? Can it be racism both ways?

right to fear this, but you need to know that officers fear this too, and work to prevent it.

This is a hard chapter to write. I've been involved in Corrections for seventeen years, including a year in Internal Affairs, and haven't seen a truly corrupt officer. Despite Hollywood—where I have *never* seen a CO (Corrections Officer) who wasn't evil or corrupt—or the many books by incarcerated felons, in which *every* officer is venal and evil (though they aren't the ones locked away for rape or murder unlike the authors), I just haven't seen a lot of evil in uniform.

I've seen some incompetence. And some stupidity. And a fair number of people so afraid of losing control that they come off as authoritarian bullies. I have seen officers who couldn't control their emotions in some circumstances, particularly anger and fear, and I have seen several who let their ego get involved.

A few of these are character issues. Some people, maybe most, are not cut out to do this job. We all read about a child being victimized and talk about gory revenge—but, unless you can read about the child, see and smell the mangled body, and still turn a smiley face on the perpetrator to get a confession, or treat him professionally so as not to endanger the conviction, you can't do this job. Not just a one-time act of will, either. You must do it again, and again, and again.

The other side, too: unless you can go in and take down a protester with appropriate force, knowing in advance it is filmed, knowing that whatever you do will be claimed to be excessive, knowing, in essence that it is a set-up—unless you can do that, this isn't the job for you. You have to be able to do the right thing even if it looks wrong. And you have to always do the right thing even if the wrong thing would be very, very satisfying.

Questionable Force

In seventeen years working jails and a year in Iraq, I have seen one excessive use of force, and it took me two months to figure out that it was excessive and why. In a big brawl, one of my officers placed his thumb over the threat's eye and advised him to comply. The threat did.

It was an ugly fight and could have justified focused blows easily. The officer used and wrote about the thumb over the eye as a pain compliance technique, which was clearly within policy. It passed review with no problems.

However, the definition of deadly force is *any* force used in a manner in which it is intended to cause death or great bodily injury. Blinding, or partial blinding, clearly would be included. The officer thought he was using a lower level than he could justify. In fact, he was using a higher level.* as defined by law. You must be able to justify deadly force.

So there was only one excessive force in my direct experience and calling that 'excessive' requires a really strict look at legal definitions.

Force will be used. If someone is offering violence to another or to you, it will require force to stop the threat unless he changes his mind and chooses to comply. There may be too little time to try anything other than force. If someone is violating other people's rights and refuses to stop or leave, he must be made to stop. That requires force.

It's a complex dynamic, however. We don't get to pick who will resort to violence, or where, or when, or who the victims will be. We

* It makes me cringe to see a martial arts or self-defense instructor teach pressure points using the handle of a knife, or a knife specially designed to press points instead of deploying the blade. The sentiment may be noble, but the legal reality is that you are using a 'deadly weapon.'

don't get to choose which officer will be the first to show up, or what tools he or she will have in the patrol car.

If I haven't stated it explicitly, here it is: Any force situation is dangerous. You could be hurt, crippled, or killed. You could be exposed to diseases you don't want to think about. You could also lose, and for many officers, that would destroy their self-image and cause more harm than any physical injury. All officers know this on some level and deal with it differently.

Not all officers stay in great shape and have years of experience working rough streets with good trainers and partners. Not all have advanced degrees in counseling or are fluent in all the languages spoken on their beat. Not all have spent years honing their skills off-duty in good martial arts classes or spent years applying tactics in war zones. Not all, maybe not even most, can stay calm and make good decisions when they are scared to death. Even the best officers may get the ugly call at the end of a sixteen-hour shift, when they are hungry, and tired, and cold.

Ideally, the perfect officer with the exact needed skills and equipment would always answer a call from a complainant who was an excellent observer with a lot of information, to deal with a perpetrator who didn't really want to hurt someone.

That doesn't happen. The dynamic of a force situation is a roll of the dice in terms of who the threat is, what the complainant can explain, and which officer (the grizzled veteran with years on CNT or the fresh rookie on his first call as primary) responds.

So here's the ugly, unstated truth about most uses of force: The officer uses force when he starts to get scared (of injury or losing control of the situation). He uses as much force as he or she feels is needed to control the fear. The force stops when the fear stops.

Those questionable uses of force that I have seen? Almost all were merely officers who got afraid before I did or got more scared than I did. From their points of view and reports, the force that they used was prudent, restrained, and justified. From my point of view, I think I could have handled it at a lower level or talked it away entirely.

That in no way means that I'm right. Officers are human and one of the endearing human traits that many have is a very inaccurate assessment of their own abilities. In most cases, meat-eaters burn away a lot of their misconceptions through trial and error. Not all ego can be great armor against learning. Some of the least effective officers I have ever seen were convinced that they were great communicators.

No matter how many fights they wound up in, or how much hate and contempt they got from criminals and even fellow officers, the bad officers couldn't seem to see how bad they were.* A failed communication became a 'great fight.' A lost fight becomes an epic in the telling later. Most of the officers in this category aren't aware enough to realize how other officers avoid them.

Several officers from a local Police Department have confided that if a particular officer from a nearby agency answers a call for assistance, they will cancel the request. They would rather deal with a dangerous situation alone than have this officer 'help.' That is possibly the most damning thing I have ever heard officers say about another.

Excessive Force

I have wanted to . . . It's not usually the crimes, actually. I'm pretty good at not thinking about the victims and just dealing with how the threat is behaving in the moment. There's a certain personality that pushes my buttons—whiny and manipulative and entitled, both violent and cowardly. The kind of person who not only has no problems with the rapes or molestations, or the beatings that they have handed

> There are some officers to whom force is just an aspect of the job and they use it judiciously and coldly. These 'cold' officers tend to make better decisions under stress, but just describing them makes some people uncomfortable. A poor decision based on fear is often easier to understand, and more comfortable than a good decision based on reasoning. People get very uncomfortable around people who are very comfortable with force.

* The Dunning-Kruger effect is the tendency for stupid or incompetent people to overestimate themselves and the very bright to underestimate their skills.

out to the smaller and weaker, but also is offended or genuinely surprised that anyone else would care either.

The kind of person that will stick a knife in an eight-year-old girl but scream that it is inhumane that he doesn't get cable TV in jail.

Yeah, I've wanted to cross the line. The feeling usually happens in a force when I am working my ass off not to injure someone who, frankly, the world would be better off without, and he starts screaming, "I'm not resisting! Police brutality!" Usually, in my experience, the guy screaming, "I'm not resisting!" is kicking and biting.

I hear, "Police brutality!" and I want to whisper, "No partner, that isn't police brutality, *this* is . . ." and give a demonstration. I haven't gone there, but I would be lying if I said I hadn't been tempted.

I have it easy. Sort of. Working corrections, I spend a lot of time with perpetrators. I spend very little time with innocent victims. I rarely see the fear and the pain. I never have to put a child into a foster care system because it is so much better than leaving the kids where they are. I rarely have to try to hear the story of a brutal crime through tears.

Excessive force happens at a confluence of two things—the officer's character and the circumstances.

Circumstances first. It's an emotional job: The crimes, the victims, the long stretches of boredom, and the surges of fear. Few people can maintain their best judgment under those conditions.

In some instances, the people you are interacting with may be attempting to provoke a response—insults and threats are common. You get used to them, but you don't quit hearing them.

Mixed signals about societal expectations can be very confusing—you are expected to do a job that includes dragging people in handcuffs to a patrol car and you are supposed to do it without hurting anyone's feelings. You are told to treat everyone equally, but when a very special person is arrested, your boss (and his boss and her boss) may all appear to make sure that this person is treated a little more equally than everyone else. You are told simultaneously to show initiative but not to do anything that doesn't already have a lot of case law supporting it.

Character, probably the most important single factor in who will be a good, average, or bad officer. It is possible for someone to do something badly because he or she doesn't know how to do it well. It is also possible for some officers to do something badly in exactly the same way as a result of who they are. One is a training issue, the other a character flaw. One is a relatively easy fix. The other may not be fixable.

This problem hits a lot of buttons in our society. The word "flaw" is very judgmental, and that is frowned on. The idea that some people might not be able to learn something seems clearly discriminatory and possibly even elitist.

These buttons exist side-by-side with other facts that are rarely challenged yet are just the same things in different words. All people are different. Personalities are defined as the collection of character traits that last over time. It is okay to say that everyone has a talent (though some seem to very clearly be without) and it is sort of okay to say that everyone has a weak spot . . . but when it extends to 'certain people are incapable of certain things,' we glitch.

Theoretical example: Look at a rookie police officer who uses excessive force. It may be a training issue in that he lacks the skills to handle a threat at a lower level. It may be an experience issue in that he doesn't have the confidence in himself to handle things the softer and riskier way. Those are both fixable.

However, he may also be prone to panic, and when the fear kicks in, he lashes out in a blind flurry. Or he just may be mean. Those are character issues and harder to fix, if they are fixable at all.

One of the problems is that in an actual incident mistakes or bad behavior can look exactly the same regardless of source. A rookie with training issues can be an asset given time and effort and experience. The same rookie with a character flaw will be a detriment and a danger to everyone for as long as he has access to victims.

It's similar on the criminal side. Every human being has criminal impulses. It would be cool to have instant gratification and if it weren't for this stupid conscience, and this nagging, quixotic belief in the humanity of others, we could go to town, baby! Tailgaters would quickly disappear from the highways.

Relatively few act on the impulses. A smaller number have no hesitation. What would be an impulse in one person is just the way things are in another—the humanity of their victims doesn't even register . . . and you get a career violent criminal.

So, which things are character and which are training? How much of the self-help industry is based on attempting to train away problems that are deeper than knowledge? If someone believes that they are largely jellyfish adrift and controlled by events (what psychologists term an external locus of control) can you really just teach them to take control of their lives and be assertive?

(This hits another snag in the discussion—there are deeper levels of teaching, some of which can affect character, but often not reliably or it doesn't last. Or people will say or even believe that their character has changed, but their behavior doesn't. Buyers beware.)

How sure do you have to be to declare something a character flaw? When do you take away an officer's gun?

Again, in most lines of work, the difference might not matter much. But in a profession where the person will be subject to high levels of stress and must make quick high-stakes decisions under that stress, a character that freezes or overreacts can get a lot of people hurt.

Where things get really interesting is when circumstances and character collide. Bad stuff happens, the officer loses control . . . and then something else will happen. Maybe an investigation, maybe merely the reaction of the officer's peers. A bad action (or any action) will have consequences, even if it appears that nothing happens.

Maybe no one knows, no one tells, no one cares. As if 'nothing' happened. In that case, the officer and his own conscience will work out whether his actions were 'really' wrong.

Maybe it is seen and reported and the officer gets the very clear message that this behavior is unacceptable and will not be repeated.

Maybe it is seen and reported and investigated and the investigation is so poorly handled that the officer comes to see the disciplinary process as essentially random. Worse than being left to his own conscience, he is left with the fundamental belief that he might be punished for things he didn't do, or not punished for things that he did, that doing a good or bad job is equally irrelevant to how his agency will respond.

The most effective shaping force on an officer who makes a mistake, does something wrong, or does a good job is the reaction of the other officers whom he respects. If the core line officers in an agency are tight and good officers, a bad officer will be chilled out until and unless he changes his ways.

In a big agency, sometimes even bad officers can find their cliques, self-righteously attaching themselves to those who fail in the same way. Timid officers hang with other timid officers and convince themselves that they are the conscience of the agency. Overly aggressive officers hang together and convince themselves that everyone else is wimpy. Insecure officers who try to act tough sometimes band together . . .

> It started in Hawaii and traveled to Oregon—a group of officers, all men, and almost all much shorter than average, who decided that if criminals were going to have their gang, officers could too. Thus was born the "Brotherhood of the Strong," a collection of officers, with small man syndrome trying to emulate the people they were supposed to watch, and control.
>
> It didn't end well. After a publicized case of clearly excessive force, each of the officers was soon out of the agency.

Unnecessary Force

Far more common in my experience than excessive force are incidents where force wasn't necessary at all. For the most part, these are NOT matters of training and skill. It is usually a situation where the officer could or should have talked, but used force instead.

Every officer goes into the situation with the training and skill that he or she has, not the skills that we wish or expect an officer to have. When an officer makes a judgment about what level of force to apply and there is a problem, it is relatively rare for other officers to say that no force whatsoever should have been necessary.

When it does happen (and it is far more often than it should be), it is usually the result of the officer letting his ego get involved and giving

Opportunity or Means to the threat, or giving up an overwhelming tactical advantage so that the threat feels empowered to fight.

Threats frequently challenge and threaten. They work hard to maintain a manly image. They say things like, "If I didn't have these cuffs on, I'd kick your ass." Or "You come into my house and I'll kill you."

An enraged inmate in a cell may scream, yell, and threaten but unless an officer opens the cell door, the threat lacks the Opportunity element. If the officer opens the cell, the *officer* has created the Opportunity. There would have been no Use of Force without the officer's cooperation. Any resulting Use of Force was completely unnecessary and completely the officer's responsibility.

One of the classic officer survival texts, Charles Remsberg's "*The Tactical Edge: Surviving High Risk Patrol*" shows a picture of an officer who responded to challenges from a threat by taking off his weapon belt. The threat had said something like, "If you weren't wearing that gun, I'd kick your ass," and the officer obligingly took it off.

Here's the deal. I'd rather scare people than fight them. One of the purposes of weapons, and uniforms, and a grim demeanor, and flashing lights, and sirens, and tactical teams, is to *prevent* using weapons. If a threat is staring down the barrel of a gun and can see the bullet sitting at the bottom (which only seems to happen with .45s, by the way), he will probably choose not to make you pull the trigger. An officer I overheard once described the laser sight on a Taser as "something to help a criminal make an informed decision."

We use superiority—in numbers, weapons, and position—whenever we can to awe the threat into NOT making us use force. To let your ego get involved and remove an advantage is to treat this issue like a game. If force results because you made the threat feel safe enough to fight, the force was unnecessary. You caused it.

3.13 Feelings of Betrayal

Riding through Northern Iraq with Frank on a gray, dusty day, I was expounding on 'professionalism.' I was being very cool and logical (it is very good when your cool logic closely matches your experience) describing how being professional even in a fight was not only possible, but worked, making the threat easier to deal with later. I talked about how taking any of this personally made you burn out faster, how no threat should ever be important enough to get under your skin . . .

"What if it's not the crooks? Don't tell me the people you worked with never got under your skin."

He had me cold, there.

This really doesn't pertain to force, but you will want to read it, anyway.

From the outside it probably looks like there is this battle going on between the cops and the criminals. Between the forces of 'good' and 'evil' or between the 'power of the state' and 'freedom,' depending on your preconceptions. All the rhetoric about war (the "war on crime" and the "war on drugs") doesn't help change that perception. Some cops feed into that too, but not all, and maybe not most.

We expect criminals to be bad guys. We expect them to lie and cheat, to use others and to fight if they think they can get away with it. With that in mind, we get along with them pretty well. It is a wary respect. You can rarely trust a criminal, but aside from their criminality, some of them are very interesting people.

This is hard for citizens to get, as most of their exposure to criminals has not only been unpleasant—stuff stolen or destroyed, injuries, rape, or death—but also included a sense of betrayal. *The world isn't supposed to be like this. What kind of person could do such a thing?* Even people who suffer from property crimes, like burglary, feel a real sense of violation.

Knowing what criminals are allows us to accept them but be aware of their nature. Criminals can be cool people. Sharks are pretty interesting fish. There are dog whisperers, and horse whisperers, and a few officers who qualify as thug whisperers.

Most rookies come in like citizens* and are very perturbed the first

* This is one major reason for writing this book: All officers have been civilians; few civilians have been officers. The civilians need information.

time they are conned—and it happens to all rookies. An inmate or arrestee comes up with a story that triggers sympathy and the rookie cuts some slack, only to find out later it was all a lie. Business as usual.

A few don't get over it—some are clueless and will fall for con after con. It is merciful if their career is short and they quit or are fired before they can go too far and actually be co-opted into a criminal act. A few go the other way, decide never to be fooled again and become the brittle, angry, aggressive officer that will go on to have many complaints and possibly unnecessary incidents.

Most do get over it, and come to accept the job as a job and the criminals as just what they are.

Because of that, criminals rarely get under our skin. It happens, but it is relatively rare. The arrestee threatening your family can trigger a lot of emotions, but less so the hundredth or thousandth time it happens (how many citizens have had more than a hundred people swear to rape and murder their daughter, wife, and/or mother, and just said and did nothing because it was business as usual?).

It is a whole different animal if the same arrestee knows your address. But that is honest fear, not generic hate between enemies.

Simple fact is that most of the time you have to care about someone for that person to hurt you.

I do care about criminals—that's why I break up fights between inmates and risk being injured, to prevent them from hurting each other. By policy and using common sense, I could just let them fight until one lost and the other was tired, and handcuff the winner. But I don't. Most officers don't. To that extent, we care.

However, we don't believe that what they say is what they believe, and we don't consider them experts on human relations. Hearing a criminal say, "You aren't a very nice guy," doesn't pack a lot of weight. A criminal lying or setting you up or trying to hurt you is just a criminal being a criminal.

It's different when it is a colleague, a boss, or a citizen.

Bosses are the most obvious and, often, the easiest to understand. At the level of line officers, bad decisions are paid for in blood. At the management level, they are paid for in lawsuits, bad press, and lost elections. Management deals with the problems that they see. They solve those problems to the best of their ability. Sometimes the solution to those problems creates other problems elsewhere, specifically at the street level. Problems that are paid for in blood.

In section 2.9 I mentioned, briefly, that the best, safest tool for dealing with people in altered mental states, the vascular neck restraint (sleeper hold or *hadaka jime*), had been removed from most officers' policy.

In the 1980s, there were several deaths that occurred right after applications of the technique. Several, being about twelve out of literally millions of applications. There was a public outcry and media pressure and most agencies either forbid the use of the vascular restraint entirely, or classified it as lethal force. I had a manager tell me specifically, "I'd rather you shoot them than strangle them. There's a lot more case law for shootings." But a shot person is always injured and sometimes killed; a 'strangled' person is almost always fine in 30 seconds. Killings and injuries are a line officer's perspective; lawsuits and case rulings are a manager's.

Managers responded to the problem *as they saw it* because the problem they saw was the outcry. There was no outcry over the millions who woke up just fine, *some of whom might have been shot* if the only safe and effective tool was removed. The problem from the line was the opposite. We still had to deal with the same people, so what are the options now? Beat them with clubs or shoot them. The management solution solved the management problem—and increased the risk to the officers and to the threats.

The officers, almost universally, felt betrayed. They wouldn't have felt bad if a criminal had tried to take their weapons away, but having it come from their own leaders . . . This is about officers' *feelings*. We have managers for a reason. We have oversight for a reason. I am authorized to use force for the sake of and in the name of the public. The public has an absolute right to know how I used it, how I made those decisions, and to deal with me if my actions are unacceptable. I am working for those citizens.

When something like this comes up, line officers want managers to stand behind us and explain to the outraged citizens, not just the force law and policy, but maybe the unintended consequences, as well.

It's a fine line that management has to walk. They are responsible for funding, and to some extent, for maintaining community support. Their decisions have impact on officer safety and sometimes that cannot be their first priority, but it is the first priority in nearly every other job in the United States.

Fellow officers are the ones that really hurt. Hollywood has gone overboard with the noble officer who turns in the bad officers and is labeled a 'rat,' or ostracized, or murdered. I've seen more from the other side: An officer crosses the line and acts like a criminal; there is a sense of betrayal and outrage from other officers who find out.

A criminal is a criminal. An officer who becomes a criminal is a traitor as well.

Cops don't like bad cops. Not just because it offends our sense of honor or because most of us believe, down to our souls, that we are the good guys and we have a responsibility to act like it. Those are emotional reasons.

If there were no emotion attached to it, we would still hate bad cops because they endanger all of us. The cop who is a dick to you hurts *your* feelings. He endangers *my* life by pissing people off. The aggressive cop who is so afraid of losing control that he jumps into a use of force as hard as he can get away with endangers his partner and all the other responding officers because they will be named in the same lawsuit that he is. And, the officer who is afraid, or doesn't know when talk is backfiring, is less help than being alone.

We can't make personalities illegal. We can't write a policy against

> Tasers are the next battlefield and an excellent example of this. As I quoted earlier, Amnesty International says, ". . . Tasers in dart-firing mode may be a preferable alternative to deadly force . . ."
>
> "May" be preferable? I tell you right now, as much as the Taser hurts, if someone had to stop me and had a choice, I'd much rather be tased than shot.
>
> Take away lower level tools and you force officers toward deadly force. That's basic math.

stupidity. Some agencies do not have a rule against cowardice in the line of duty (and one person's cowardice is another's "good judgment").

But because they are officers and you expect more from them, because you care what they think, they can get under your skin.

Citizens may be the hardest of all. Stressed, scared, angry people regress. Some start acting like toddlers. Toddlers often act like criminals (or, more probably, criminals failed to outgrow certain stages, e.g., "Mine! Mine!" not understanding or caring about others' property and throwing temper tantrums).

That means that sometimes citizens under stress start acting like criminals. Drunken citizens often try to fight, something most haven't done since junior high school. They argue, sometimes stupid arguments (ask any officer how many times he has pulled drugs out of a suspect's pocket and been told, "These aren't my pants").

That's one level, and it doesn't bother us too much in the moment. Later, when the guy sobers up and realizes what a mess he's made, that gets our sympathy.

Sometimes citizens don't understand when they have stepped through the looking glass, when they have entered a part of the world where their civilized expectations mean nothing. If a drunken college kid walks into a redneck bar or a biker watering hole and doesn't know the rules of that particular subculture, he can wind up in a world of hurt. That's just an example.

When officers show up to deal with a citizen, especially if the officers have weapons out, the citizen has stepped through the looking glass whether that was his intention or not.

The citizen shouldn't assume or expect social niceties. When things get tense, officers use communication to make things happen—it is terse and direct. As one friend put it, "I'm here to save your ass, not to kiss it."

If a fireman responds to a fire at a house, the residents don't demand that he knock on the door and wait politely for an invitation. He knocks down the damn door with an axe and you'd better not try to stop him.

When an officer gives an order, a lawful order, clear and concise, and a citizen tries to turn it into a debate on manners and demands a 'please,' the officer is not sure what game the threat is playing. He is a threat now, by the way. He has failed to follow a lawful order and is showing, at minimum, passive resistance.

But the officer doesn't know what the game is—is it just a jerk with a sense of entitlement trying to punk out the officer for his own ego? Or is it an attempt to distract the officer for another purpose?

But sometimes, sometimes, the citizen says "Thank you." That makes all the rest worthwhile.

> A Canadian citizen crossing the border to the United States at Blaine, Washington was ordered to turn off his car. That is the first thing Border Protection officers are trained to do if they suspect something. The Canadian chose not to follow the order. Instead, he demanded that the officer say "please" first.
>
> The officer repeated his order. The traveler repeated his demand for a please. The sequence was repeated three times.
>
> Then the officer advised the traveler to turn off the car or the officer would deploy OC. The traveler again demanded a "please." He got pepper-sprayed.

This incident strikes me as dick-wagging of the highest order. The officer was doing his job. The traveler decided he was going to show the public servant who was the real boss. The officer was sucked into the game.

Should the officer have said "please"? Sure. It certainly would have saved a pile of paperwork. Would it have encouraged the traveler to continue with his childish, entitled behavior? Probably. It is rare that people like this realize how much they live at the mercy of others more polite than they.

It was a lawful order and the threat was not complying. The force used was clearly commensurate with the threat—pain compliance for static resistance. Justifiable? Absolutely. Justified? Prudent? Necessary? That's your call.

3.14 Totalitarianism

I made some statements in the Introduction about totalitarianism. It is relevant and will continue to be because police officers are often accused of being a sort of Gestapo. They get told every day that they serve the state and are an instrument of evil.

> Once upon a time I was booking a very old lady into jail. She had been arrested for DUII. In her quavery voice and distinct German accent, she said, "I lived in Hitler's Germany and even the Nazis didn't send little old ladies to jail for having a little drink."
>
> They just killed you for going to the wrong house of worship.
>
> That wasn't the worst part, though. At the same time, we were booking a young lady. I don't remember the charge—it could have been anything from public indecency (streaking) to assault (spitting on someone), but was most likely trespassing, refusing to leave a business when asked/ordered. Minor charges. But she started yelling, "You tell 'em, grandma! You don't have to take this shit!" and chanting, "Fight, fight, fight!"

For her own amusement, she was trying to get an eighty-year-old woman to fight an officer. If it happened, we would do everything possible not to hurt her, but even holding her hands down could bruise old skin.

This is our common experience with protestors: They violate others' rights, whether refusing to leave private property or harassing people on public property or blocking off roads, forcing people to spend more time in gas-guzzling cars and depriving them of their right to get where they are going. They bring children, babies, and the innocent to volatile places where they intend to provoke a reaction from police. They then use the babies that they endangered as shields, excuses, or pretexts for lawsuits. They bring a mass of angry people, some of whom have taken and given classes on how to blind officers with battery acid, or cripple the horses of mounted patrols—then they have the effrontery to call it a "peace march."

Then, when they violate the license for their protest, or endanger someone, or in some other way force the officers to intervene, they begin to chant that the officers represent a police state.

> We were out on the line during a scheduled protest. The candidate that the protestors loathed had won the election—not just the Electoral College, but he was the first president elected with a popular majority since Reagan. However, that wasn't what they wanted, and what they wanted overrode the fact that the majority disagreed with them. They scheduled a protest.
>
> My job was to be out there to process any arrests that were made. At one point, the protestors decided to take over a bridge. In a town with a big river cutting through it, you can mess with a lot of people by shutting down a bridge. Rationalizations aside, messing with people was a goal. They could pretend that it was an exercise of free speech, or standing up for . . . (what? the right of the minority to win as long as it was their minority?), but in the end, it was just a mass temper-tantrum, without even the excuse of spontaneity.
>
> The protestors massed on the bridge. The officers lined up opposite. The officers took one step forward and the protesters took one step back until they were off the bridge. They wanted confrontation, but safely. Courage wasn't anymore a strong suit than civic responsibility.
>
> But as they stepped back they were chanting, "This is what a police state looks like!" The juxtaposition of the chant and the officers in black armor played well on the news. It played less well at my house.
>
> My kids told me later that mom had been yelling at the TV screen during the live news special, "No, it doesn't you stupid sons of bitches! In a real police state they machine gun your dumb asses and those of you who make it home each find a family member missing!"
>
> Did I tell you my wife was a refugee from the old Eastern Bloc?

People confuse freedom with being able to do anything they want without consequences. From that point of view, anyone setting boundaries is considered oppressive. The math doesn't work for that. The protestors, doing what they wanted to do, were interfering with other people's rights. They were oppressing the innocent. Freedom and respect for rights has to be a two-way street.

Most people can't articulate why our system is galaxies away from a totalitarian system because they have only experienced one system. Most of my in-laws lived under a police state until the fall of the Berlin wall. I have had friends and co-workers from Ceasescu's Romania. I am writing this in a Baghdad that may never recover from Saddam Hussein's reign.

In the U.S., if you riot and block traffic and break glass, you might get pepper-sprayed and may have to spend a night in jail. You can then sue, and might even get something.

In Romania, in the seventies, if you asked about getting permission to leave the country, you might go home to find your eleven-year-old daughter with her arms cut off and a note from the secret police pinned to her chest.

In the U.S., if a jail is crowded, the inmates sue and we wind up creating an elaborate matrix system so that as few inmates as possible are released and they are the ones least likely to do violence. The Warden of Rusafa No. 1 told me that in Saddam's Iraq, when the prisons got crowded in Rusafa, one-third of the inmates were marched to the top of the Ministry of Interior building and pushed off. It was cheaper, and more amusing, than shooting them.

For most officers, democracy is sacred. We take an oath and part of that oath is to defend the Constitution. The Constitution is a damned fine document and it has a lot in it—ways for people to challenge the powers of the state; checks and balances on the power of the state. Case law over time has given means of redress against the excesses of the state.

That is critical. Power has a tendency to concentrate, and those wielding power do all that they can to exempt themselves from those controls. That is the nature of power and of people.

The first amendment guarantees some of the critical elements of maintaining a democracy. Don't, for the moment, think of freedom of speech and the freedom to peaceably assemble. In my opinion, those are shorthand for the freedom to share and spread information.

I'm an idealist on this. I know that most people's political views are emotional reactions and the research is very solid that facts don't really make much difference. There is enough data out there (and opinion masquerading as data, and flat-out lies) that anyone can cherry-pick the sources that validate what they choose to believe. I know that—but I want to believe, it is an article of my faith—that truth will win out.

Information, solid information, will convince enough people in a constitutional republic to make good choices. Those choices manifest in carefully considered spending and in carefully cast votes.

Our leaders become and remain leaders by promising to do what they believe we want. When they fail to meet our expectations, we vote them out. And they leave. At the end of the Clinton administration, certain elements on one side were convinced that he would create a political emergency to declare martial law so that he could remain in power. It didn't happen. When the second Bush administration's second term ended, the same fears were expressed by different people.

It didn't happen. Martial law would require the police and military to believe that the person declaring martial law was more important than the constitution. That's not going to happen, not just to keep some politician in power.

There have been incidents of martial law.* Like using force to stop violence, it is an unfortunate fact that the democratic process and taking steps to ensure everyone's rights are protected is a time consuming system. When the choice is between protecting the process (rights) and protecting lives, lives win. That is why militaries and police units defend democracies, but are not themselves democracies. They need to be able to respond faster than voting allows.

* Federally, very few, if any, since President Lincoln's attempt during the Civil War challenged *Ex parte Milligan,* 71 U.S. (4 Wall) 2 (1866). States, however sometimes have equivalent laws, such as the "state of public health emergency" invoked after Hurricane Katrina destroyed effective civil authority.

If voting fails, don't be surprised if many of the people taking the most active role in restoring democracy are the police and military.

Like most people who wear a badge, I didn't have a lot of respect for civil lawyers or the American Civil Liberties Union. It seemed that this organization put enormous effort and money into protecting criminals, keeping violent people on the street and ensuring that criminals had access to defenseless victims.

Then I went to a country that for thirty years had no one to defend basic rights. I see the value now.

Many criminals aren't particularly violent. Some are, when it is safe to be violent. But almost universally, criminals are manipulative and don't care about others. That inability to care largely defines a

> You need to know your role in the news. You are neither a witness nor a consumer of the news. You are a product. The news media is a business, and they are selling YOU. Do you send a check to the nightly news show? Does what you pay for the morning paper begin to cover the cost of the paper and ink? No. The source paying for the news is the advertisers and they pay on the understanding that the media outlet can provide a guaranteed number of people who will be exposed to their ads.
>
> The purpose of the media is not to inform or educate or expose. Its purpose is to entertain, to 'hook' enough readers, watchers, or listeners to make a profitable base for the products advertised. Truth is secondary to this. If enough information is thrown out fast enough, only the people directly involved will catch the inaccuracies. Value of information is secondary to revenue. As I write this, very few people have any solid idea of what is being done to resolve an economic crisis, but even in Iraq everyone knows that Michael Jackson, an entertainer, is dead.
>
> It's about the money. You are the product. As long as they are not caught and even when caught in a lie, as long as they are not successfully sued, the truth doesn't matter. The truth doesn't pay the bills.
>
> The First Amendment is about the freedom of information and of communication. It is critical to a democracy . . . but be skeptical. There is no automatic guarantee of truth in freedom.

criminal personality. Being manipulative is just second nature when one lacks empathy.

Like many cops, what I saw was manipulative users who would create a situation, and then either con or hire an attorney to try to get money or try to hamstring an agency to make crime easier and safer.

That's not what the civil attorneys and the ACLU see. They see the enormous power of the state ranged against the paltry resources of a single person, often poorly educated and without wealth or resources. Someone needs to defend those who cannot defend themselves. That's completely true and noble. However there is no system, so far, so noble and well designed that it can't be twisted by users.

As I said, having now spent some time in a country that had no equivalent of the ACLU, I've come to appreciate them more. Force has to be used sometimes, and it has to be used by people for the good of the community. As long as that dynamic exists, the people tasked to use that power must be watched. Sometimes, they may need to be reined in. I just hope, with this book, that those decisions are based on understanding the problem and not an emotional reaction to a situation hyped to increase audience and advertising revenues.

Without strong constitutional safeguards, safeguards that are jealously guarded by both the government and the people, democracy is an extremely vulnerable institution. People like to be right, and it takes enormous strength to recognize that we might be wrong. It takes enormous strength to afford others the respect to voice contradictory opinions. A primary goal of any despot is to silence those voices. Trying to silence those voices, either through state-sponsored censorship or the soft, warm, and 'benevolent' censorship of political correctness, is a sure sign of a totalitarian agenda. It may not be conscious, but if people can be fired from jobs, particularly government jobs, for either speaking in favor of gay rights or voicing doubts about global warming, the people doing the firing have the beginnings of a totalitarian agenda.

The danger to democracy is that this is a one-way slide. Intolerance, from any political ideology, can be voted into practice. They can then make it illegal to vote the intolerance out. The people working for freedom, affording others the right to argue, debate, and potentially convince, must win *every time*. The totalitarians only need to win a single election.

Baron de Montesquieu in *The Spirit of the Law* noted that more than any other system of government, a republic required virtuous people. "*This virtue may be defined as the love of the laws and of our country. As such, love requires a constant preference of public to private interest; it is the source of all private virtues, for they are nothing more than this very preference itself.*

This love is peculiar to democracies. In these alone the government is entrusted to private citizens."

Democracies do not create good people. Democracies rely on good people. If we lose our virtue, our handful of shared core beliefs, beginning with the Bill of Rights, we will lose our Republic.

Enough preaching.

3.15 Interview with Loren Christensen

Lots of officers don't particularly care to share their stories, except for sometimes over a beer or around a bonfire. For many, writing is a chore and reminiscent of interminable reports.

Loren Christensen is the exception. He's a retired line officer, Defensive Tactics instructor, veteran who worked as a Military Policeman in Saigon during the Vietnam war, an iconic martial artist (once named one of the "20 Toughest Men in the World", which makes him blush when you mention it), and a prolific writer. The man likes to write and he knows how to communicate. He has been there and done that on a level that would make many people cringe, cry, or lose bladder control. He'll get a special mention in the bibliography—for now, just know that Loren is special, a combination of experience and communication skill that is rare.

He can't, however, follow instructions. I wanted war stories. He asked for specific questions. What it turned into was a recap of many of the points in the book, including where he disagreed with me and where he called me on my agenda. Here it is.

Miller: When or if: looking at what you were expected to teach by the academy and knowing it wouldn't work for most of your officers.

Christensen: There is a story in which an aikido student criticized the art to the teacher saying that it would never work in a real fight. The teacher just nodded as the student talked on and on. When he finally stopped the aikido teacher said, "Son, aikido works. I've seen yours and it doesn't."

All defensive tactics work, but many officers, for a host of reasons have trouble with them or opt not to use them at all. This is because officers in many agencies are given limited hours to train. When I went through the academy, we received eight hours of judo flips. Eight hours! As I write this, I have been training in the martial arts for 44 years. Even with those many years "on the mat," there are techniques I don't do well, lots of them, in fact. So if after 44 years I have moves that I wouldn't trust on the street, how can an officer be expected to do something after only a few hours?

Miller: What news stories really burned you because they just didn't get it?

Christensen: Here are a few stories that reveal total ignorance of how things work in violence and chaos: [Rory, I left out 'why' they're ignorant. Figured you could elaborate on it if you want to use any of them].

- Criticisms because an officer shot the suspect who was only armed with a knife.
- Criticisms because the police shot a suspect who was only trying to run them over with a car.
- Criticisms because it took five officers to wrestle the suspect into custody.
- "Officer shoots woman for jaywalking." A headline that ignores the fact that when the officer stopped the woman to tell her to cross at the corner, she pulled a gun on him.
- Criticisms for shooting the armed suspect so many times.
- Criticisms that the rioters wouldn't have torn up downtown if the police hadn't confronted them.
- Criticisms for racial profiling.
- Criticisms that officers are afraid to come into certain communities.
- Quick judgments about police action when those complaining haven't a clue as to what happens to the human body under great stress.

Miller: Are there officers who strike you as being just as ignorant about fighting as civilians? What kind of officers are they and how do they maintain their ignorance?

Christensen: I would say that the majority of officers I knew were ignorant about fighting. Because I worked in Portland, Oregon where backup was usually five minutes away, at the longest, most officers never had a one-on-one, knockdown, drag-out. In other words, their fighting skill had never been tested because they always had help. Many were good police officers but were simply not prepared to fight *mano y mano* with someone alone. Fortunately, most never had to.

Too many officers hate to train in defensive tactics. They would rather spend hours shooting holes in paper targets than learning how to control resisting people. Shooting is sexy; bending arms and legs hurts.

This issue was and still is absolutely amazing to me. Officers need to understand that DT skills and legitimate confidence in their skills make their job so much easier—and safer. Too many officers get hurt and use excessive force because they lack these two elements.

Officers spend eight hours a shift driving and, in the course of their career, engage in far more empty hand confrontations than just about anything else they do, except for writing reports. Nevertheless, they get the least amount of training in driving, and in defensive tactics.

Miller: Has damned if you do, damned if you don't ever felt like the norm?

Christensen: It's always the norm. It's one of the big frustrations, and one of the things that made it sometimes difficult to go out every day to serve and protect.

For example, I know of an officer who did a tracheotomy on a woman and saved her life. Saved her life! Then she sued the department because the emergency procedure left a small scar on her neck.

Another example: An officer responded to a bank robbery. As he ran toward the bank entrance, the holdup man exited and gut-shot the policeman. The policeman clutched his midsection and toppled to the cement, uttering "Goddamnit!" as he fell. A nearby witness later filed a complaint with internal affairs because the officer had used a bad word.

On a much smaller scale, I know a Portland officer who got an internal affairs complaint because she was always frowning. So she began smiling more. Then—you know where I'm going here—she got a complaint because the citizen thought her smile was inappropriate.

Oh yes, there were times when I would say, "Screw the public," though the feeling never lasted longer than the next hot call to help someone. Cops always go no matter how bad the press and no matter how many criticisms are directed at them. They go because doing so has been ingrained in them and, perhaps most importantly, there is within them that innate quality that that is the thing they do. They go.

Miller: What is the one thing that civilians don't get about it?

Christensen: They have no concept of the job's complexity and resultant stress, and the absolute dedication that most officers have to serve and protect.

Secondly, they don't consider, and most likely don't care, that it's our police officers who must go toward violence, that horror that everyone else runs from it.

Imagine for a moment that you're a police officer riding in a car on a beautiful, balmy evening, when dispatch informs you that there are three armed career criminals at the corner of Third and Main. They have already shot two people, they say they will not go back to prison, and they will kill the first police officers who arrive. So what do you do?

You hurry to get there! You even activate your lights and siren so you can get through traffic faster. And what do you see as you get near the intersection? Everyone running away from the three men.

Case in point: My partner and I received a call to a high-rise where a man, armed with a shotgun, was stalking the halls after pumping eight rounds into his psychiatrist's face (he reloaded once). We got the call and then we sped to get there, as did five or six other units.

When we arrived, we literally had to push and shove our way through, against hundreds of panicky people running and screaming out of the building.

Years later, I was reminded of that when I saw that photograph of a lone fireman, a very frightened looking young man, going up the stairs of one of the Twin Towers on September 11, when other people in the photo were running down the steps.

One other issue: Civilians have no grasp of how hard it is to handcuff someone who doesn't want to be cuffed. I've been in hundreds of resist-arrest situations, so many that most just blur together in my mind. That said, there were two that occurred early in my police career that made it clear that not all hard-to-handle resisters are burly Northwest loggers.

One was with a pregnant 15-year-old girl and the other was a person in his 70s. Neither wanted to be arrested and both resisted with all they had, and incredibly, they had a lot. Now, if I could have smashed them in the face with my fist, the confrontation would have been over. But the resistance they offered didn't justify that level of force. Still, they stiffened their limbs and thrashed around violently, both with amazing speed and strength. Both confrontations lasted for ten minutes, or so, and both were exhausting. Fortunately, we eventually handcuffed them without injury to anyone.

Miller: How many uses of force have you had and if that was broken into seconds and minutes, how much time have you (or anybody, really) spent with real world violence?

Christensen: I was in law enforcement for 29 years, first as a military policeman in the army, with a year of street duty in Saigon, Vietnam, and then as a city cop in Portland, Oregon. My experience with uses of force includes everything from simply forcing someone's stiffened arms behind their backs to grappling with people on sidewalks, in streets, on stairs, in bathroom stalls, in riots, in phone booths, and in cars. I also had a few toe-to-toe slug-it-out situations. Combined, these incidents number in the high hundreds.

Quickie use-of-force situations last mere seconds, while some of the longer ones can go anywhere from three minutes to twenty. Some riots in which we fought constantly, with intermittent breaks, lasted for hours (a couple of them for 15 hours or more).

I once fought a friend for 30 minutes behind a grocery store where we both worked (the friendship was a tad strained after this, made even more awkward because we were dating sisters). This was just before I started training in the martial arts. It was a slugfest from the beginning to the end.

I get your question and where you're going with it. I suppose the same thing can be asked of other things, too, i.e.: We trust people to guide 3,000-pound motor vehicles through insane traffic conditions, though how many total minutes have any of them spent functioning in real world emergencies? Has any motorist with 30 years driving experience had more than 15 accumulative minutes of braking hard, accelerating hard, swerving hard, etc., to avoid a nasty crash? I'm not sure if it's the same concept. Maybe.

SECTION 4: ABOUT YOU

It's all about you, baby.

Here's the deal—you can read and study forever but if you can't use the information, it is worthless. Worse, if you can't apply this, I've failed as an author, and I hate that.

In this last section, I'm going to talk about you. Specifically, what you should have learned that might be new; how and why communities interact negatively with officers and how it could be better; and applying this perspective if you ever have to interact directly with an officer.

4.1 What You Didn't Know Before

The purpose of the book is to help the average citizen understand how officers see force and how in many cases, officers have no choice (under the duty to act) or bad choices (cutting slack is literally betting their lives) in some of the decisions made. The United States, despite some hype and stories, is a largely affluent and peaceful place to live. We are inundated with reports of violence constantly, but violence itself is relatively rare.

This has several important effects, things that affect you as a citizen, juror, and voter:

- Any use of force appears shocking to the uninitiated
- People who make judgments about a use of force they were not involved in usually have access to information the officer did not have (such as a diagnosis for unusual behavior) and almost always have far more time to analyze information
- They also lack information the officer had. They did not see, hear, feel, smell, or sense what the officer did
- Stopping violence or potential violence is a separate issue from 'justice'—motive and mental competency are keys to determining the level of criminal culpability, but are irrelevant to whether someone must be stopped before they hurt somebody.

I hope, and this may be the hardest sell in the book, that when you see or read of an officer using force you have a better understanding of the circumstances that drove it and the rules the officer works under. It is easy to react on an emotional level and demand change. It is rarely productive.

Change must be driven by understanding. It might be terrible, unfortunate, and tragic when a scared and confused man refuses to drop his knife and is shot. To be upset is a completely valid reaction, but completely emotional. Would the results have been better if the scared and confused man had been allowed to keep his knife?

A vague feeling that there should have been a better result is meaningless without a concrete tactic that would have worked better.

Every use of force hurts somebody. There will never be a violent person stopped from doing a violent action who is cool with it. (Not in the moment. There have been a few with a few days of perspective who thanked me for what I stopped them from doing.)

The questions to ask yourself, when evaluating a situation are:

1. What was the alternative to force being used?
2. What were the possible and probable consequences of those alternatives?
3. Was the option used the lowest level of force that would have safely worked? And remember, in this question, to be careful to distinguish between pain and injury.
4. Did the officer follow the rules?

That is the line that officers must follow and that citizens must demand. If we lived in a world where force was never necessary, none of this would matter and this book would just be an intellectual exercise. We don't live in that world and we can't pretend that we do.

Governmentally and societal sanctioned force is an immense power. You can't wish it away and you can't evaluate it from a utopian ideal. So we write rules for it and hold the people to those rules. Not to our feelings. And, if necessary, we change those rules but from understanding and insight, not from a vague sense of dislike.

4.2 Police Relationships with the Community

There is a trend, something I see in parenting and in aspects of legislation and very much when questions of force and behavior arise.

It is easier to blame good people than bad people. It always bothers me, and I can't count the number of times I have seen it: parents scold children not for something they did, but for something they didn't prevent another child from doing. "You're the oldest. We expect more from you. You shouldn't have let little Mikey play with those matches."

It is cowardice, pure and simple. The good kid, the smart kid, the mature kid will hang his head and promise to do better. That's easy parenting. Confront the bad kid directly and he may face you down, argue, even fight or run away. Punishing the good kid is easier and feels like you are doing something.

It is the exact same dynamic when agencies are sued for injuries resulting from high-speed chases or shootouts caused by criminals. You sue a criminal and he laughs at you and goes on with his lifestyle. His drug profits are undocumented and can't be seized, and it might be physically dangerous to actually try to collect. It's much easier, safer, and more profitable to sue the police who were reacting to the situation the criminal created. Same dynamic. Cowardice under the illusion of doing something.

This hits another trend that officers are very familiar with—the neighborhood meeting. After many highly publicized incidents, "community organizers" appear and call for meetings to teach the officers sensitivity and put them in touch with the community.

Many of these officers spend more hours in the community than the so-called community representative. The officers know what goes on that no one talks about, who the victims are, and often who the perpetrators are. They see the mothers of the victims cry. Still, the organizers hold meetings and try to teach the officers how hard it is to live in this area, sometimes an area where the officer spends more waking hours than anywhere else.

Not once have I heard of this being reversed, the officers taking charge of the meeting and telling the people what they know about what really goes on. There are occasional 'gang information' meetings or discussions, but for fear of hurting feelings, officers don't stand up and tell the truth:

"We care more about your community than you do and we can prove it. We aren't putting together words and meetings, we are shedding our blood, every day, trying to stop your son from raping her daughter; trying to keep your nephew from selling drugs to that man's cousins. But you know this. You also know who is doing the bad things, and you are afraid of them. Not only do you not report the crimes, but you help to hide the criminals. Too many of you would rather see a rapist or murderer get away than be seen talking to us.

"You say it's our job, but we aren't psychic. We can't catch criminals if their victims protect them. You need to stand up. You need to tell the bad guys you will not accept the badness and then work with us to put a stop to it.

"You can pretend all you want that these bullshit meetings help. They don't. They just make you feel better."

Sorry for the vent and I know you could read the emotion in that, but it is very true. If you are losing your neighborhood, *you* need to take it back. The cops will help. But you can't give away and sell out your own neighborhood and count on the cops to somehow magically prevent things from going downhill. The math doesn't work.

I know this is hard. The criminal community is held together by blood and friendship ties (though friendship is far more a matter of convenience with criminals than in the civilized world), and these ties go deep into the neighborhood. Often, when the victims are your friends and relatives, so are the perpetrators. When officers come in as outsiders, it seems that they are trying to get you to turn on one of your own. In a way they are, but only if you identify more closely with the criminals than with the victims. Because, and hear this well, it's not about the officers versus the bad guys. It never has been. It's about the bad guys versus the victims.

HARD TRUTH #11

It's not about the officers versus the bad guys. It never has been. It's about the bad guys versus the victims.

When and if you forget that and you refuse to help catch someone, you aren't "standing up against the 'man,'" you are turning your back on sometimes hundreds of victims and you are sending a message loud and clear to the criminals: "We like you just the way you are, my special snowflake. Your predation is just fine here."

THE LAST HARD TRUTH, #12

Communities get the kind of crime that they tolerate.

So, what can you do as a citizen, a neighbor, and a community member? This is a JFK thing and it boils down to "Ask not what your country can do for you . . ."

The next time there is a community meeting with the police, focus on what you can do, on how you can help the police. Give that a try.

4.3 Dealing with an Officer

I probably should have amended that to dealing with a scared officer, but the line is pretty thin.

One of my friends attempted to design a class to instruct people on how to interact with police. He was told bluntly that people should be able to do or say anything they wanted and it was up to the officer to tell if they were kidding. This group was willing to expend no effort on their own behalf and willing to rely on the psychic powers of the average officer to determine whether a death threat was real or a brandished gun was a toy.

Hopefully, among the things you've gathered so far is that officers don't have psychic powers, or bullet resistance, or superhuman strength. They are ordinary people who have to make sometimes extraordinary decisions. Hopefully, I've put you inside their heads a little bit.

That doesn't do any good, not unless you choose to apply for the job and take the oath. Unless . . .

Chris Rock has a great video, "How Not to Get Your Ass Kicked by the Police." There's a lot of racial stuff in it, but the advice is solid.

Here's the bottom line: Be an adult.

If an officer confronts you, especially with a weapon out, that is no time to be playing stupid little kid games or trying to show your manhood. He will make force decisions based on what you do and what you do not do. Be mature and intelligent, and help him make the best possible force decisions.

If an officer tells you to do something and it is safe to do it, do it. Yes, we all prefer to be asked. Yes, the officer may not sound very friendly. The officer may also be covering an access point for a Secret Service detail inside (who will not respond well to an unexpected entrance), or be holding a place for an ambulance on the way, or trying to hear on the radio where the armed man was last seen.

If being told what to do triggers a "You're not the boss of me!" reaction, things might not end well.

Don't get defiant. Think about it. If the officer is there for a reason and that reason involves you, somebody thought what you were doing warranted police intervention. I highly advise you to not tell the officer what he can and can't do. For one thing, he's almost certainly been in this situation more than you have. Second, he knows pretty well what he can and can't do—and a lot of that will be based on your behavior, including your defiance. It is one of the things that will go to show Intent when he writes his report. Third, he may be required to do something, such as take you into custody, that you think he can't do. Don't give him the impression that he has to use force to do it.

Officer: Sir. You're under arrest. Pease turn around and let me handcuff you.
You (quiet, polite tone)**:** Officer, I haven't done anything wrong.
Officer: That's possible, sir, and they may be able to straighten it out downtown, but I do have to take you in. Turn around, please.
You: (complying) Okay, but this is a big mistake.

OR:

Officer: Sir, you're under arrest. Please turn around and let me handcuff you.
You: Fuck you! I know my rights! I want a lawyer!*
Officer: You'll have a chance to arrange for a lawyer when you get to the precinct. (At this point, the officer is probably already putting one hand on his Taser or OC.)
You: Fuck you! I'm not going! (At this point, any fast motion will probably trigger an immediate and unpleasant response from the officer).
Officer: Get down on the ground now!

If you have to be defiant, don't be stupid about it. Argue, if you absolutely have to, but *show the officer your hands*. If the officer says, "Show me your hands!" and you say, "No," you have given the officer no choice but to assume that you have a weapon ready to deploy. This is so stupid—right up there with checking for gas leaks with matches—it shouldn't even need to be said, but it happens. Being defiant about something stupid can escalate a verbal situation to deadly force for childish, immature ego.

If the officer ever uses the magic phrase, "For your safety and mine, I need you to . . ." do it. That is a solid signal that the officer perceives this as an issue of safety and the officer will absolutely use force if you do not comply.

4.4 An Outside Perspective

Jeff Gaynor wrote something profound on the roots of people's feelings and expectations for police officers:

> Being good though is very powerful in our culture and therein lays the problem. Consider why God is God. Do you realize that

* The Miranda warnings are one of those rights that "everyone knows" wrong. You have a right to have an attorney present if you are under arrest and you are being questioned. In other words if an officer is just talking to you in your home, or you have voluntarily gone to the station to 'answer a few questions,' you have no right to an attorney. If you are under arrest and no one is asking you about a crime, you have no right to an attorney. You always have a right to keep your mouth shut, however.

it is because he is good (or supposed to be)? Other cultures have no problem at all with fairly evil deities (Shintoism comes to mind, and what about Baal and sacrificing children?), mostly because they were modeled on natural forces which are capricious. A specific Western (and Christian) take is the requirement that God be good and this is why people who have spiritual crises have them the way they do: if a loved one dies or there is poverty, etc. in the world, how can that be reconciled with a good God?

Said differently, morality in some sense even trumps divinity as nowadays people refuse to believe in God at all since they cannot reconcile that there is evil with this fact. This little digression puts into light, I hope, why requiring people to be "good" in our culture can quickly get out of control. Perhaps we need a return to the concept of being virtuous, rather than being good. Meaning, one tries to act with virtue in all situations, but it is a human striving to overcome his/her foibles. This accepts an essentially tragic view of life, which is all but extinct today.

What I am saying is that the requirement that cops be the good guys is a bottomless pit. Not even God has managed to live up to this cultural expectation. Perhaps Marc overdid it a bit, but I very much see why he feels LEOs are between a rock and a hard place. Primitive human behavior under stress is about as far off the mark from being good as can be imagined.

THE HARD TRUTHS

#1) *The only defense against evil, violent people is good people who are more skilled at violence.*

#2) *In a truly totalitarian environment where the authorities cannot only kill, but have control over who finds out about it and control over the means to respond, the populace is helpless.*

#3) *In the extreme moment, only force can stop force.*

#4) *Sometimes an officer will be forced to make a decision in a fraction of a second on partial information where the BEST choice will leave a corpse, a widow, two orphans, and someone who needs therapy.*

#5) *You can't achieve a dream by dreaming.*

#6) *There will never be a simple formula to give clear answers to how much force is enough. Force incidents are chaos and you can't write a cookie-cutter answer to chaos.*

#7) *If you become injured or exhausted while at a certain level of force, it is a sure sign you were using too low a level. You are losing! If you keep using something that is already not working, you will fail utterly. This is not a game.*

#8) *Experience will change you.*

#9) *Knowing what to do is not the same as doing it.*

#10) *Surrendering is a learned skill.*

#11) *It's not about the officers versus the bad guys. It never has been. It's about the bad guys versus the victims.*

#12) *Communities get the kind of crime that they* ***tolerate.***

GLOSSARY

active shooter scenario. A situation in which one or more threats are actively engaged in killing with guns, such as the Columbine school shooting.

adrenaline loop. Sometimes very scared people do the same thing over and over again even when it is not working. This behavioral looping is a form of freezing.

APD. See Antisocial Personality Disorder.

Antisocial Personality Disorder (ADP). A persistent pattern of behavior characterized by unwillingness to follow rules or social norms; low impulse control; irresponsibility; aggressiveness; deceit; and a lack of remorse.

BJS. Bureau of Justice Statistics.

booking. Sometimes called "Intake" or "Reception." The place where newly arrested people are first brought into the jail.

Circumstances. In a use of force, those qualities in the environment or that develop during the fight that may justify a lower or higher level of force. Relevant circumstances might include a sudden assault, inability to escape or get help, or the fight happening in a hazardous environment.

Civilian (or Citizen's) Review Board (CRB). A group unaffiliated with a police agency tasked with overseeing or checking the Internal Affairs process.

CNT. See Crisis Negotiation Team.

compliance. When a threat or potential threat voluntarily does what is required.

confrontational simulations (ConSim). A training method where officers are put through realistic scenarios with actors and safe training weapons.

ConSim. Confrontational Simulations.

contained. The threat is considered contained when he can no longer access victims. He has been denied Opportunity. See Opportunity.

control. In a use of force, control is forcing the threat to do what is required or forcing the threat to stop undesirable actions.

Corrections. That division of Law Enforcement tasked with keeping convicted inmates and those awaiting trial in secure custody.

Crisis Negotiation Team. (CNT). Used to be called "Hostage Negotiations Team" and then someone noticed that even when there wasn't a hostage, people needed to be talked down.

CRB. Citizen Review Board or Civilian Review Board. Usually referred to as "The Crib."

deadly force. Definition differs by statute in many places and it is one of those things where a small change in wording can have a profound effect on meaning. Generally, deadly force is any force that (could/will/likely to/intended to/did) cause death or serious physical injury.

duty to act. Citizens have the right to say, "I don't wanna." That right is not extended to certain professions. Whether codified by policy or law, certain people, notably emergency services personnel on duty, are forbidden to ignore certain situations. Under normal circumstances, an officer cannot ignore a violent felony, or a paramedic called to the scene of a medical emergency cannot refuse to treat.

Defensive Tactics (DTs). Hand-to-hand skills ranging from simple handcuffing to unarmed self-defense taught to officers. Some agencies and jurisdictions include armed self-defense under the term "Defensive Tactics."

DTs. Defensive Tactics.

EDP. Emotionally Disturbed Person.

EMS. Emergency Medical Services.

Emotionally Disturbed Person (EDP). A catch-all phrase for anyone acting significantly strange or who appears to be in an altered state of consciousness. Extreme drug reactions, mental illness, and extreme emotional levels can all mimic each other. EDP is a non-diagnostic label that the person is in one of these altered states.

Enforcement. That division of Law Enforcement tasked with enforcing the law.

entry team. Specialized group that goes into high-risk buildings, such as drug houses, to affect arrests, serve warrants, or rescue hostages.

EVOC. Emergency Vehicle Operator Course.

excessive force. Using a level of force higher on the force continuum than can be justified.

Excited Delirium. A rare and sometimes fatal condition of unknown etiology. Often associated with stimulant abuse (hence the old term, 'cocaine psychosis.') Common symptoms include profuse sweating, extremely high body temperature, inability to articulate, and often violence including self-destructive behavior. In practice, people in excited delirium rarely respond to pain or reason and sometimes show unusual strength, speed, and endurance.

factors. In a use of force, factors are the differences between the officer and the threat that may justify a higher or lower level of force. Common factors include differences in size and strength, fighting skill, or numbers of officers and threats.

Force Continuum. Though quickly being abandoned as a teaching tool or policy requirement, many agencies have and still do codify force into levels ranging from simple presence on the scene to deadly force. That range of options makes a force continuum.

Hep-C. Hepatitis C.

HIV. Human Immunodeficiency Virus.

HNT. Hostage Negotiation Team. See *Crisis Negotiation Team.*

IA: Internal Affairs. IAD is Internal Affairs Division; IAB is bureau; IAU is unit.

Intent. One of the three factors that make an immediate threat. Intent is the threat's desire to do something wrong.

Internal Affairs (IA). The unit within a law enforcement agency tasked with investigating complaints of misconduct.

interrogation. A formal and systematic questioning of a suspect under the assumption that the suspect will not wish to divulge information.

interview. Gathering information by asking questions. Compare with *Interrogation.*

jail. A facility for holding accused criminals awaiting trial and misdemeanants, people convicted and sentenced to less than one year. See Prison.

LEO: Law Enforcement Officer.

levels of resistance. A rough guide to the type of problem a threat represents.

Less-Lethal. A designation for munitions that are designed to be incapacitating or cause pain without a high risk of serious injury e.g. rubber bullets.

Lop. An under-performing officer. See *ROAD.*

means. One of the three factors that make an immediate threat. Means is the threat's ability to do something wrong. A handgun or knife, for instance, is the means for a lethal threat. Fist and boots are means for an ominous or assaultive threat.

meat-eater. A very active or aggressive officer.

Mobile Data Terminal (MDT). The computer networked into many patrol cars.

MVA: Motor Vehicle Accident.

NPD. See Narcissistic Personality Disorder.

Narcissistic Personality Disorder (NPD). A persistent pattern of behavior characterized by fantasies of wealth, fame, or power; an expectation of special treatment; lack of empathy; and exploitation of others.

oleoresin capsicum (OC). Pepper spray.

opportunity. One of the three factors that makes an immediate threat. Whatever means the threat has, he must be able to reach his victim with the means.

prison. A facility for holding convicted felons, criminals sentenced to more than a year. All felons go through jail on the way to prison. Misdemeanants do not go to prison.

profiling. Drawing conclusions from observable facts.

psychotic break. This is not a psychologist's term but a cop's term for someone who has become temporarily irrational, often caused by extreme emotional distress.

Reasonable Person/Officer rule. The test of whether someone with equivalent training and experience would have made a similar decision in the same situation.

restrained. In a use of force the threat is considered restrained when he or she can no longer attack effectively, e.g., by the application of handcuffs. Restraining a threat denies *means*. See *Means*.

ROAD. Retired on Active Duty. Derogatory. See *Lop*.

rookie. A new officer.

subcaliber. Many munitions, designed for force-on-force training, such as confrontational simulations, are designed to be 'subcaliber.' Thus, the training ammunition is too small to work in duty weapons, and it is impossible to accidentally load duty ammunition into the training weapons.

SWAT. Special Weapons and Tactics. There are now a lot of different names, and thus a lot of different acronyms for Tactical Teams. SOG is Special Operations Group. ERT is Emergency Response Team . . . you get the idea.

Taser ©. A Conducted Energy Device that fires two probes attached by wires into the threat. The Taser then sends 50,000 volts but only 2.1 milliamps down the wires. Very little damage. Incredible pain.

threat. The common law-enforcement term for someone who might require force to be used.

Totality of the Circumstances (TOC). All of the details of a given situation that drive an officer's force decision.

unnecessary force. Using force when force was not necessary, or force arising from a situation that the officer helped to create, such as by supplying *opportunity* or *means*.

USBP. US Border Patrol.

use of force (UofF). An incident where an officer uses physical skills ranging from holding to shooting, to control an individual or situation.

WNL. Within Normal Limits.

ANNOTATED BIBLIOGRAPHY OF FURTHER READING

What follows can never be exhaustive. In eighteen years working in the field I've taught or been taught material on this subject well over a hundred times. There are uncounted emails, discussions, pamphlets, and class handouts that gave some perspective or a new insight. Newspaper articles and reports written by officers with hands still shaking. Lectures and speeches by civilians with definite points of view.

The ones listed were important and memorable, for the most part, and hopefully easy for people outside of the job to find. A few (many of the articles without comments) gave me a statistic I used in the book without direct experience. I've never personally polled Civilian Review Boards or checked with every state to see what they teach at the Academy, for instance.

If anything in the book piqued your interest, especially if you disagree vehemently with what I've written, read some more. Dig for sources. Always keep your mind open, especially to people who disagree with you, but never invest everything in one source. Not even me.

Adams, Ronald, Thomas McTernan, and Charles Remsberg. *Street Survival: Tactics for Armed Encounters*. San Francisco: Calibre Press, 1980.

With Remsberg's *The Tactical Edge, Street Survival* was the bible for patrol officers for many years. Lots of good advice, lots of insight into how to get the job done as safely as possible, and to keep your own ego from getting you killed.

Allen, Bud, and Diana Bosta. *Games Criminals Play*. Roseville, CA: Rae John Publishers, 1981.

Aimed primarily at corrections, but the authors give a good account of how criminals manipulate. You should read this book if you interact with criminals and, possibly, before you read books written by criminals.

American Psychiatric Association. *Diagnostic and Statistical Manual of Mental Disorders, Fourth Edition (DSM IV)*. Washington, DC: American Psychiatric Publishing, Inc., 2000.

It is what it is. DSMs are the authority on mental illness. Because they say so, that's why.

Amnesty International. "Amnesty International's Continuing Concerns About Taser Use." *Amnesty International*, 2006.

Lots of groups have agendas. Lots of groups do press releases. Please, please, please, don't just read the press releases. Read the articles themselves, and be skeptical. They may work hard to make the article say something the facts don't support.

Anderson, Dennis. Director of the documentary *Ultimate Survivors—Winning Against Incredible Odds.*, 1991.

Several stories of officers who have survived when they shouldn't have. The title describes it well. My agency used the section on the murder of Linda Lawrence and the subsequent fight with her murderer as a training film.

Anderson, Elijah. *Code of the Streets: Decency, Violence and the Moral Life of the Inner City.* NY: W. W. Norton & Company, 2000.

I got a lot of insight from this one on a lot of different levels. Read it.

Artwohl, Alexis, and Loren Christensen. *Deadly Force Encounters: What Cops Need to Know to Mentally and Physically Prepare for and Survive a Gunfight.* Boulder: Paladin Press, 1997.

Loren Christensen has also written several books solo on defensive tactics, gangs, martial arts training . . . The kind of things that you wish an experienced cop would write.

Blum, Lawrence W. *Stoning the Keepers at the Gate: Society's Relationship with Law Enforcement.* NY: Lantern Books, 2002.

In my opinion, Dr. Blum missed with this one. *Stoning the Keepers* is a scholarly work, exhaustively sourced. There is enough in his bibliography to keep an interested reader going for some time. His agenda, and the emotions behind the scholarly tone, didn't sit well with me. It's good stuff, it's accurate, but it felt like a voice crying in the wilderness, "You don't understand." If you've done the research, or shed the blood to understand, the book will validate what you already understand. Because of that, it will reach officers but few civilians.

Capra, Frank. Director of the film, *It's a Wonderful Life.* Hollywood, CA: Liberty Films, 1946.

If you're into this sort of thing, I guess it's okay. Presented here as an example of a movie almost everyone has seen, and in which most don't even blink when an officer attempts to shoot a drunk in the back for running away. Some even point at the movie as an example of simpler, happier times. Times have changed.

Chasnoff, John. "A Review of Civilian Review" *Synthesis/Regeneration* 39 [Winter 2006].

de Secondat, Charles, baron de Montesquieu. *The Spirit of Laws.* Chicago: *Encyclopaedia Britannica,* 1955.

An old book and sometimes tough to read, but important. Originally published in 1748, it reminds us that a Republic was not always the base line and delves into the special problems, needs, and processes of monarchies, aristocracies, dictatorships, and democracies.

Geller, William. *Deadly Force: What We Know—A Practitioner's Desk Reference on Police-Involved Shootings.* Police Executive Research Forum, 1992.

I'm not aware of anything done since Geller that matches the sheer scope of research. It is a compilation of statistical fact with analysis of what we knew, and what we didn't know, about officers using deadly force.

Gilmartin, Kevin. *Emotional Survival for Law enforcement: A Guide for Officers and Their Families.* Tuscon: E-S Press, 2002.

Describes the cycle, as well as the resulting psychic wear-and-tear of a daily transition from a job that requires constant vigilance for survival and safety to trying to be a husband or wife, mother or father.

Gladwell, Malcolm. *Blink: The Power of Thinking Without Thinking.* NY: Little, Brown and Company, 2005.

Describes some of the mechanisms your brain uses to make quick decisions

Grossman, Lt. Col. Dave. *On Killing: The Psychological Cost of Learning to Kill in War and Society.* NY: Little, Brown and Company, 1995.

A pioneering work on the psychology, particularly the difficulty and aftermath, of human-on-human violence. Though the research is drawn primarily from military experience, much of it applies to police work.

Hall, Christine, MD, and Sgt. Chris Butler. "TR-03-2007 National Study On Neck Restraints in Policing." *Canadian Police Research Centre,* June 2007.

Any technique that gets a lot of attention can be labeled as dangerous or extreme. Sometimes real scientists get together and check it out. This is one such study.

Kane, Lawrence, and Kris Wilder. *The Little Black Book of Violence.* Wolfeboro NH: YMAA Publication Center, 2009.

Not a little book at all. The two Seattle-based martial artists and authors have amassed a lot of information on some very bad things. The book is designed, expressly, to help young men make informed decisions about what fighting is, and what is worth the fight.

Kenny, Dr. John M., Captain Sid Heal, and Captain Mike Grossman. "The Attribute-Based Evaluation of Less-Than-Lethal, Extended-Range, Impact Munitions." *Applied Research Laboratory, Pennsylvania State University,* February 2001.

Technical, but points out that in this emerging technology not everything works quite the way it is supposed to.

Kirschman, Ellen. *I Love a Cop: What Police Families Need to Know.* NY: Guilford Press, 1997.

Details the emotional changes that affect most rookies as they learn the job and become veterans. It can be hard on families, too.

Klinger, David. *Into the Kill Zone—A Cop's Eye View of Deadly Force.* San Francisco: Jossey-Bass, 2004.

Concentrating exclusively on Deadly Force, David Klinger presents a broad range of what officers experience. He never says anything is just one way—he shows why different people choose to become officers at all, and many different experiences of training. Klinger writes about how various officers thought about taking a life before, during, and after the event and how it affected their lives. It's a wide range, people. Some folks were crushed, and some were hardly affected, maybe even validated. Klinger lets the officers tell it in their own words.

Johnson, Jeffry L. "Use of Force and the Hollywood Factor." *2007(4) AELE Mo. L.J. 501 Special Articles Section* April 2007

What most people believe to be true about violence and police actions and responsibilities is learned from movies and television. It is possibly the greatest cause of the gap between officers and the communities they serve.

Line of Duty.com. *Murder of Georgia Deputy* (video).

The dashboard camera film, with research, interviews, and commentary of Deputy Kyle Dinkheller being murdered.

Miller, Rory. *Meditations on Violence.* Wolfeboro, NH: YMAA Publication Center, 2008.

An overview of my thoughts on the nature of violence.

Reaves, Brian A. PhD. "State and Local Law Enforcement Training Academies, 2006." *Bureau of Justice Statistics* (February 2009).

Remsberg, Charles. *The Tactical Edge.* San Francisco: Calibre Press, 1986.

One of the classics of officer survival. Written by cops and for cops at a time when the profession was in transition. Violent crime was high, less lethal options, like OC and Taser, were less common and less reliable. The book is packed with vital information.

Rock, Chris. *How Not to Get Your Ass Kicked by the Police,* Chris Rock Show, HBO, n.d.

It's funny, but it is so right it hurts. Obey the law. Be polite. Don't hang out with stupid people.

Tueller, Dennis. "How Close is too Close?" *SWAT Magazine,* March 1983.

The first publication to point out that sometimes bringing a gun to a knife fight didn't work out so well. The genesis of the "21-foot rule" that a threat with a knife can cross seven yards and slash, or stab, before the average officer can draw a weapon.

U.S. Constitution and Bill of Rights.

Read it, at least once a year.

U.S. Supreme Court Graham v. Connor, 490 U.S. 386 (1989).

U.S. Supreme Court Tennessee v. Garner, 471 U.S. 1 (1985).

INDEX

BOOKS FROM YMAA

6 HEALING MOVEMENTS
101 REFLECTIONS ON TAI CHI CHUAN
A WOMAN'S QIGONG GUIDE
ADVANCING IN TAE KWON DO
ANCIENT CHINESE WEAPONS
ANALYSIS OF SHAOLIN CHIN NA 2ND ED.
ARTHRITIS RELIEF: CHINESE QIGONG FOR HEALING & PREVENTION, 3RD ED.
BACK PAIN RELIEF: CHINESE QIGONG FOR HEALING & PREVENTION 2ND ED
BAGUAZHANG
CARDIO KICKBOXING ELITE
CHIN NA IN GROUND FIGHTING
CHINESE FAST WRESTLING: THE ART OF SAN SHOU KUAI JIAO
CHINESE FITNESS: A MIND / BODY APPROACH
CHINESE TUI NA MASSAGE
COMPLETE CARDIOKICKBOXING
COMPREHENSIVE APPLICATIONS OF SHAOLIN CHIN NA
CONFLICT COMMUNICATION
DUKKHA: A SAM REEVES MARTIAL ARTS THRILLER
DUKKHA REVERB: A SAM REEVES MARTIAL ARTS THRILLER
DUKKHA UNLOADED: A SAM REEVES MARTIAL ARTS THRILLER
EIGHT SIMPLE QIGONG EXERCISES FOR HEALTH, 2ND ED.
ENZAN: THE FAR MOUNTAIN
ESSENCE OF SHAOLIN WHITE CRANE
ESSENCE OF TAIJI QIGONG, 2ND ED.
FACING VIOLENCE
FIGHTING ARTS
INSIDE TAI CHI
KATA AND THE TRANSMISSION OF KNOWLEDGE
LITTLE BLACK BOOK OF VIOLENCE
LIUHEBAFA FIVE CHARACTER SECRETS
MARTIAL ARTS ATHLETE
MARTIAL ARTS INSTRUCTION
MARTIAL WAY AND ITS VIRTUES
MEDITATIONS ON VIOLENCE
MIND/BODY FITNESS: A MIND / BODY APPROACH
THE MIND INSIDE TAI CHI
MUGAI RYU: THE CLASSICAL SAMURAI ART OF DRAWING THE SWORD
NATURAL HEALING WITH QIGONG: THERAPEUTIC QIGONG
NORTHERN SHAOLIN SWORD, 2ND ED.
OKINAWA'S COMPLETE KARATE SYSTEM: ISSHIN RYU
PRINCIPLES OF TRADITIONAL CHINESE MEDICINE
QIGONG FOR HEALTH & MARTIAL ARTS 2ND ED.
QIGONG FOR LIVING
QIGONG FOR TREATING COMMON AILMENTS
QIGONG MASSAGE —FUNDAMENTAL TECHNIQUES FOR HEALTH AND RELAXATION, 2ND ED.
QIGONG MEDITATION: EMBRYONIC BREATHING
QIGONG MEDITATION—SMALL CIRCULATION
QIGONG, THE SECRET OF YOUTH
QUIET TEACHER
ROOT OF CHINESE QIGONG, 2ND ED.
SHIN GI TAI—KARATE TRAINING FOR BODY, MIND, AND SPIRIT
SHIHAN TE: THE BUNKAI OF KATA
SIMPLIFIED TAI CHI CHUAN 24 & 48 POSTURES
SUNRISE TAI CHI
SURVIVING ARMED ASSAULTS
TAE KWON DO: THE KOREAN MARTIAL ART
TAEKWONDO BLACK BELT POOMSAE
TAEKWONDO: A PATH TO EXCELLENCE
TAEKWONDO: ANCIENT WISDOM FOR THE MODERN WARRIOR
TAEKWONDO: DEFENSES AGAINST WEAPONS
TAEKWONDO: SPIRIT AND PRACTICE
TAI CHI BALL QIGONG: FOR HEALTH AND MARTIAL ARTS
TAI CHI BOOK
TAI CHI CHIN NA: THE SEIZING ART OF TAI CHI CHUAN
TAI CHI CHUAN CLASSICAL YANG STYLE (REVISED EDITION)
TAI CHI CHUAN MARTIAL APPLICATIONS
TAI CHI CHUAN MARTIAL POWER
TAI CHI CONNECTIONS
TAI CHI DYNAMICS
TAI CHI QIGONG, 3RD ED.
TAI CHI SECRETS OF THE ANCIENT MASTERS
TAI CHI SECRETS OF THE WU & LI STYLES
TAI CHI SECRETS OF THE WU STYLE
TAI CHI SECRETS OF THE YANG STYLE
TAI CHI SWORD: CLASSICAL YANG STYLE
TAIJIQUAN THEORY OF DR. YANG, JWING-MING
TENGU: THE MOUNTAIN GOBLIN, A CONNOR BURKE MARTIAL ARTS THRILLER
TRADITIONAL CHINESE HEALTH SECRETS
TRADITIONAL TAEKWONDO
WESTERN HERBS FOR MARTIAL ARTISTS
XINGYIQUAN, 2ND ED.

DVDS FROM YMAA

ANALYSIS OF SHAOLIN CHIN NA
ADVANCED PRACTICAL CHIN NA IN DEPTH
BAGUAZHANG 1,2, & 3 —EMEI BAGUAZHANG
CHEN STYLE TAIJIQUAN
CHIN NA IN DEPTH COURSES 1: 4
CHIN NA IN DEPTH COURSES 5: 8
CHIN NA IN DEPTH COURSES 9: 12
EIGHT SIMPLE QIGONG EXERCISES FOR HEALTH
THE ESSENCE OF TAIJI QIGONG
FIVE ANIMAL SPORTS
INFIGHTING
KNIFE DEFENSE—TRADITIONAL TECHINIQUES AGAINST DAGGER
MERIDIAN QIGONG
NEIGONG FOR MARTIAL ARTS
QIGONG FOR HEALING
QIGONG MASSAGE—FUNDAMENTAL TECHNIQUES FOR HEALTH AND RELAXATION
SHAOLIN KUNG FU FUNDAMENTAL TRAINING 1&2
SHAOLIN LONG FIST KUNG FU: BASIC SEQUENCES
SHAOLIN SABER: BASIC SEQUENCES
SHAOLIN STAFF: BASIC SEQUENCES
SHAOLIN WHITE CRANE GONG FU BASIC TRAINING 1&2
SIMPLE QIGONG EXERCISES FOR ARTHRITIS RELIEF
SIMPLE QIGONG EXERCISES FOR BACK PAIN RELIEF
SIMPLIFIED TAI CHI CHUAN
SUNRISE TAI CHI
SUNSET TAI CHI
SWORD—FUNDAMENTAL TRAINING
TAI CHI ENERGY PATTERNS
TAIJI BALL QIGONG COURSES 1&2—16 CIRCLING AND 16 ROTATING PATTERNS
TAIJI BALL QIGONG COURSES 3&4—16 PATTERNS OF WRAP-COILING & APPLICATIONS
TAIJI MARTIAL APPLICATIONS: 37 POSTURES
TAIJI PUSHING HANDS 1&2—YANG STYLE SINGLE AND DOUBLE PUSHING HANDS
TAIJI PUSHING HANDS 3&4—MOVING SINGLE AND DOUBLE PUSHING HANDS
TAIJI SABER: THE COMPLETE FORM, QIGONG & APPLICATIONS
TAIJI & SHAOLIN STAFF - FUNDAMENTAL TRAINING
TAIJI YIN YANG STICKING HANDS
TAIJIQUAN CLASSICAL YANG STYLE
TAIJI SWORD, CLASSICAL YANG STYLE
UNDERSTANDING QIGONG 1: WHAT IS QI? • HUMAN QI CIRCULATORY SYSTEM
UNDERSTANDING QIGONG 2: KEY POINTS • QIGONG BREATHING
UNDERSTANDING QIGONG 3: EMBRYONIC BREATHING
UNDERSTANDING QIGONG 4: FOUR SEASONS QIGONG
UNDERSTANDING QIGONG 5: SMALL CIRCULATION
UNDERSTANDING QIGONG 6: MARTIAL QIGONG BREATHING
WHITE CRANE HARD & SOFT QIGONG
YANG TAI CHI FOR BEGINNERS

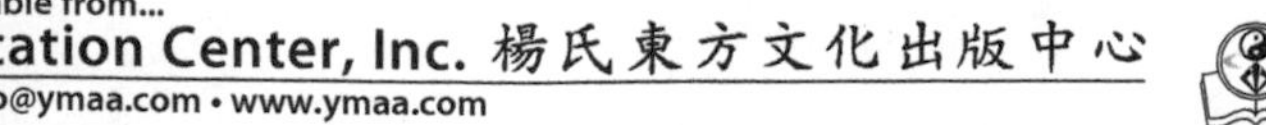

Printed in the USA
CPSIA information can be obtained
at www.ICGtesting.com
JSHW022335140824
68134JS00019B/1493

9 781594 392436